YOUNG WRITERS

OVER THE MOON

OXFORDSHIRE

Published in Great Britain in 1996 by
POETRY NOW
1-2 Wainman Road, Woodston,
Peterborough, PE2 7BU

All Rights Reserved

Copyright Contributors 1996

HB ISBN 1 86188 098 7
SB ISBN 1 86188 093 6

Foreword

The *Over The Moon* competition was an overwhelming success - over 43,000 entries were received from 8-11 year olds up and down the country, all written on a wide variety of subjects. Reading all these poems has been a painstaking task - but very enjoyable.

Many of the poems were beautifully illustrated. This just emphasises how much time, effort and thought was put into the work. For me, this makes the editing process so much harder.

I hope that *Over The Moon Oxfordshire* highlights the diversity of today's young minds. I believe that each of these poems shows a great deal of creativity and imagination. Many of them also express an understanding of the problems, socially and environmentally, that we are all facing.

The poems that follow are all written on different levels, and some are more light-hearted than others. With a considerable variety of subjects and styles, there should be something to appeal to everyone.

Sarah Andrew
Editor

CONTENTS

Ashbury Church of England Primary School

Tom Hearn	1
Claire Stehle	2
Nick McDiarmid	2
Robert Irvine	3
Oliver Warren	3
Natasha Mills	4
Abigail Dillon	4
Andrew Crouch	5
Laura Hayes	5
Andrew Treadwell	6
William Evans	6
Jorgina Lowry	7
Justine Best	7
Elizabeth Dagnall	8
Rebecca Moulding	8

Aston Rowant School

Jennie Bright	9
Tom Bright	9
Katie Griffiths	10
Matthew Ward-Barber	10
Philip Hodge	10
Aneke Orth	11
Teresa Garratty	11
Steven Cook	12
Johnny Boulton	12
Roxanne Smith	12
Gemma Walker	13
Jenna Green	13
Hannah Allworth	13
Holly Jones	14
Craig Merrell	14

The Blake C E Primary School

Stephanie Harwood	14
Rachel Stace	15
Michael Mullin	15
Jenna King	16

	Ben Hockney	16
	Daniel O'Dell	17
	Tiffany Wishart	17
	Stacey Forward	18
	Nathaniel Miles	18
Caldecott Primary School		
	Kayleigh Provins	19
	Lauren Rossiter	19
	Laura Oultram	20
	Graham Morris	21
	Emily Constance	22
	Lucy Bough	22
	Katherine Newbold	23
	Laura Wells	23
	Emily Warder	24
	Natalie Kathryn Allred	24
	Alison Trotman	25
	Melissa Head	25
	Kimberley Furze	26
	Alice Warder	26
	Lucy Smith	27
	Michael McCormack	27
	Simonne Blair	28
	Cheryl Harris	28
	Anthony Gleeson	29
	Chris Webb	29
	Donna Collins	30
	Liam Bramall	30
	Jenna Brown	30
Edward Feild CP School		
	Jamie M White	31
	Tim Archard	31
	Laura Pollard	32
	Hannah Pearce	32
	Holly Lambourne	33
	Gareth Siret	33
	Joanne Eagle	34
	Camille Dunkley	35

	Zehra Chudry	35
	Kate Broadbent	35
	Jade Laforest	36
	Carima Ghani	36
	Ali Hakimi	37
	Lauren Davis	38
	Hayley Carter	39
	David Stanmore	40
Freeland CE Primary School		
	Jodie Evans	41
	Claire Watson	41
	Charlotte E Barrow	41
	Lorna Moir	42
	Mark Crocker	42
	Jamie Lawes	42
	Thomas McNeil	43
	Sebastian Delaisse	43
	Jamie Barlow	43
	Jade Berry	44
	Rebecca Leggett	44
	Robert Atherton	44
	Lucie Watson	45
	Audur Alexandersdottir	45
	Eleanor Atherton	46
	Richard Wood	47
	Kate Wylie	47
	Rebecca Mutlow	48
	Faye Bunting	48
	Ian Moore	48
Glory Farm School		
	Jamie Warner	49
	Joshua Thomson	49
	Gary Venters	50
	Martin Winstone	50
	Naomi Calderon	51
	Lyndon Davis	51
	Kashia E Adams	52
	Danielle Prpa	52

	Daniel Hewer	53
	Claire Ford	53
	Andrew Morris	54
	Donna Butler	54
	Tina Matthews	55
	Wesley Lewis	55
	Lauren Spencer	56
	Danielle Reading	56
	Marc Abbey	57
	Daniel Wood	57
	Stacey Moody	58
	Joanna Wilkinson	58
	Sam Burnand	59
Kingham CP School		
	Gemma Tomalin	59
	Scarlette Matthews	60
	Sophia Alidina	60
	Robert Shackelton	61
	Alice Bagnall	61
	Emily MacAvoy	62
	Morwenna Baylis	62
	Edward Blake	63
	James Dawkes	63
	Mattea Cottle	64
	Emily Aldridge	64
	Peter Fox	65
	Zoe McIntyre	65
	Harry Shepherd	66
	Natalie Edwards	66
Mill Lane Primary School		
	Leanne Cadet	67
	Marcus Hare	67
	Laura Joanne Stevenson	68
Millbrook CP School		
	Laura Farhan	68
	Jessica Dancy	69
	Luke Talboys	69

Our Lady's Convent Junior School, Abingdon		
	Nancy Homewood	69
	Elizabeth Barclay	70
	Jessica Edwards	70
	Christopher Byrne	71
Rush Common School		
	Lisa Brown	72
	Hayley Davies	72
	Jenna Calcutt	73
	Beccie Jones	74
St John's School, Banbury		
	Sadie Ekers	74
St Joseph's RC Primary School, Carterton		
	Laurence Whyatt	75
St Mary's Prep School, Henley		
	Sarah Barton White	76
	Abbie Millward	76
	Catherine Robinson	77
St Nicolas School, Abingdon		
	Jessica Davis	77
	Richard Scott	78
	Catherine Workman	78
	Simone Minal	79
	William Drury	79
	Richard Rawling	79
	Joseph Derek Barton	80
	Guy Bennett	80
	Michael Wallace	81
	Hannah Salisbury	82
	Lauren Moore	83
	Richard Baker	83
	Alice Alphandary	84
Shenington CE Primary School		
	Alex Crosse	84
	Charles Saunders	85
	Nicholas Dexter	85
	Nicholas Porter	86
	James Dexter	86

	Ben Young	87
	Toby Lee	87
	Roberta Bullingham	88
	James Wasley	89
	Ricky Zito	89
	Laura Wood	90
	Alexandra Thomas	90
	Francesca Nunneley	91
	Claire Pettit	92
	Philippa Wilkinson	92
	Zoé Crosse	93
	Lucy Poulton	93
	Rosemary Pollard	94
	Richard Edwards	95
	Henry Lane	95
	Michael Cullen	96
	Rebecca Johnston	96
	Edward Allsopp	97
	Guillermo Sanchez	98
	Laura Gaydon	98
	Sophie Tisdall	99
	Jenny Berresford	99
	Robin Wilcock	100
	Jennifer Allott	100
	Joe Cooper	101
	Jason Slade	101
Uffington Primary School		
	Kirsty McHardy	102
	Louise Hibbard	102
	Louise Sworn	103
	Sophie Bowsher	104
Wantage CE Junior School		
	Caroline Woodhouse	105
	Rebecca Partington	105
	Hannah Ewing	106
	Christopher Alder	106
	Richard Rees	107
	Cheryl Shepherd	108

Stuart Anderson	108
Lydia Haddrell	109
Andrew Bellis	109
Sally Scholes	110
Helen M Isserlis	111
Joe Spray	112
Nicholas Clinch	112
Laura Cavanagh	113
Jeremy Russell	113
Lynsey Pickett	114
Henry Callaghan	114
William Pattison	115
Victoria Barrett	115
Amy Pickett	116
James Herkes	116
Faye Richardson	117
Jonathan Coxall	118
Victoria Alice Green	118
Mark Cottrell	119
Catharine Birch	119
Amy Bridle	120
James Ridgwell	121
Andrew Donovan	121
David Easton	122
Jocelyn Donnelly	122
Thomas Malton	123
Douglas Frost	123
Kirsty Jones	124
David Stephen Finch	124
Matthew Hallam	125
Ben Cole	125
Steven Vaux	126
Caroline Moore	127
Mark Harris	128
Helen Oakes	129
Ben Carter	130
Shaun McNamara	131
Auriol Proudfoot	131

Kate McIntyre	132
Alison Barber	133
Elizabeth Berrett	134
Naomi Ryland	135
Mark Clements	136
Daniel Humphries	136
Timothy Kennington	137
Jessica Rolls	137
Laura Bowles	138
Stevie Rutter	139
Kieran Wheeler	140
Stuart May	141

AS HIGH AS THE CLOUDS

A balloon came to our school one day
On Friday the ninth of May
The men laid it down on the ground
In a great plastic mound.

The burner was fired
It began to rise
I thought something was wrong
So I closed my eyes.

Of course it was alright
But it gave me a fright
A killer balloon
As big as the moon.

But I jumped in the basket
And cut the rope
I was determined
That I could cope.

I went higher and higher
As I re-fuelled the fire
Then we started to go down
And sunk towards the ground.

I landed in a stream
And I felt rather mean
Because I'd stolen a balloon
As big as a moon.

Tom Hearn (10) Ashbury Church of England Primary School

LIFE BEHIND A FOSSIL

A fossil in its normal sense,
is a rock or stone with a pretty dent.
But behind the imprint is life and movement,
when you look closely and dream,
of dinosaurs and things so fierce,
it really makes you scream!
I close my eyes and try and imagine . . .
I jump as a Tyrannosaurus Rex,
snaps his jaw shut tight,
then he leaps and starts a fight,
the victim is a Stegosaurus,
he falls down and lashes his tail,
gives a wail . . .
and dies.
Then I look into the T-Rex's eye,
Then my tummy
goes all funny
and I heave a sigh. Pheewwwwwwwwwww

                        It was just a dream . .
                             or was it?

Claire Stehle (9) Ashbury Church of England Primary School

THE MOON IS A BALLOON

Harnessed to fly
At night it prepares for flight
High above the sky so gracefully as it floats
Through the night sky
So white and elegant it floats through
the sky
Like a feather in the wind.

Nick McDiarmid (10) Ashbury Church of England Primary School

WAR BALLOON

War balloon black,
War balloon white,
War balloon never goes out at night.
War balloon shot it bursts into flames
People think pilot's truly insane!
War balloon bomb,
War balloon gun,
Driving it mustn't be fun.
War balloon filled with deadly gas
Floating around in empty mass.
It's a larger version of a hot-air-balloon
To be inside it you would surely swoon.
War balloon black,
War balloon white,
War balloon never goes out at night.

Robert Irvine (10) Ashbury Church of England Primary School

THE SKY

In the clouds somewhere
the balloon soars higher and higher
clouds drift like smoke
as you see the bustling land below
the people are ants scurrying about

But that is not important the sky is my kingdom
I am the king and the clouds are servants

But as I land I know now
that I am not the king
but I know that in the air
I am the master in the sky.

Oliver Warren (11) Ashbury Church of England Primary School

THE STORM

A tiger pounds through the misty forest
Dark clouds fill the air
A thunder storm starts
The tiger now elegantly runs
To a shelter with glaring eyes
Bang! a clap of thunder
Spindly trees breaking
Shades of brown and green
Camouflages together
Swaying long grass in the wind.
Now it's all dark and quiet
All except the whistling wind.

Natasha Mills (10) Ashbury Church of England Primary School

DRIFTING

Drifting through the air
in a big hot air balloon.
Swaying and tilting
on the breeze.
The stripes and colours
on the balloon
show up as bright as the moon.
Lifting slowly higher and higher
flying above the telephone wires.
Slowly, slowly we go back down,
then we land with a sudden bump,
Pack away, then we eat our lunch.

Abigail Dillon (11) Ashbury Church of England Primary School

THE HOT AIR BALLOON

The hot air balloon.
As tall as a tower of cloth,
I get in a giant basket
with a big flame over my head.
The man presses a button
and we go up
the ground below gets smaller and smaller.
Moving along
it's like the balloon is in its own land
below I see once again
a village like a little toy town,
the fields are like a big lump of straw.
I then see a little flame
signalling where to land
we go down lower and lower
then a thump and bang we are down.

Andrew Crouch (10) Ashbury Church of England Primary School

A BALLOON IN THE SKY

A balloon in the sky
Nearly as high as the clouds
Floating along like a bird
Looking for a place to rest or land
Gently drifting along the sky
The flame burning high
Filling the balloon with nice hot air
But when the flame dies
The balloon gently falls to the ground
The balloon will fly again up in the sky
With its flame burning high.

Laura Hayes (11) Ashbury Church of England Primary School

A BALLOON FLIGHT

Up in the sky
The balloon flies high
The balloon rides the wind
Across the countryside.

As far and as high
the balloon flies by
The balloon seems to run
across to the red hot sun.

The balloon comes down
To land on the ground.

Andrew Treadwell (11) Ashbury Church of England Primary School

HIGH AS A BIRD

Up in the sky
High as a bird
In a balloon
High in the sky
The burner burning
Getting higher every minute
Hot air makes it go up
It goes to the moon
Some big, some small
Little people on the ground
Small people in the balloon
Small as ants
Flying is so fun
Better than a plane
It is so nice to fly.

William Evans (8) Ashbury Church of England Primary School

UP UP WITH THE WIND

Up up with the wind goes the yellow balloon
Past the stars the cloud and the moon.
Up up through space goes the yellow balloon
How I wish I could fly to the moon
How I wish I could fly to the moon in a yellow balloon.
It would be such fun to be in a yellow balloon
If you look down and see all the tiny villages
How I wish I could fly to the moon like a balloon
Or even a bird or a jet or a plane
Just to be in the sky or be able to fly
But then I think I'll never be able to fly.

Jorgina Lowry (8) Ashbury Church of England Primary School

FLYING HIGH

Flying high up in the sky
The wind blows through my hair
The people down below look like insects
I am above high as can be
going past a flying bird.
Its wings are moving fast
Coming down as slow as can be.
Down below the field is free
and we land so carefully
I miss the sky flying high.

Justine Best (11) Ashbury Church of England Primary School

HIGH IN THE SKY

High in the sky or drifting low,
come on I want to go.
Soaring so high, soaring so low,
Drifting where I want to go.
Coming in to land
We are going to hit the ground
People crowding round me
by the sea.

Elizabeth Dagnall (9) Ashbury Church of England Primary School

HIGH IN THE SKY

Wisping through the open sky
Flying flying up and high
over valleys
under trees
Feeling for the open breeze
Soaring up
Soaring down
Watching out and saying
'Wow'
The air is cold
cold and wet
let out the air
going down
gently touch the clear green ground.

Rebecca Moulding (11) Ashbury Church of England Primary School

RECIPE FOR A SHARK

Take two rows of razor-sharp teeth and stir well
for ten minutes in the blood of fifteen bats.
Add two round eyeballs and leather tough dorsal
fin and mix in a bowl.
Cook it at gas mark 4 until fin is a dark blue
colour.
Take the teeth of ten dinosaurs and sprinkle all over
a strip of lizard kin.
Stuff with the bones of a herring and a cod.
Leave it in the freezer to set for 3 hours then wait
for a stormy night so you can tape it to the TV aerial.
Let a bolt of lightning strike the aerial.
You'll probably have a power cut but your shark
will be completed!

Jennie Bright (11) Aston Rowant School

A RECIPE FOR FRANKENSTEIN

Get a cauldron hot
and a bolt or two,
green sludge
and a hair or two
an old coat
a fat goat
Mix, mix
Bubble bubble
Now it's time for some real trouble.

Tom Bright (9) Aston Rowant School

CINQUAIN

Whale
Gracefully
Calling, swimming, spurting
Singing in the water
In the sea

Katie Griffiths (11) Aston Rowant School

RECIPE FOR AN ALIEN

Take an X-file potion (the X-file 'Pilot' is best)
Add big black bug eyes (Rhino beetles if possible)
Don't forget to sieve world domination
Sprinkle egghead pieces (two eggs are better
than one)
leave for a week or two.
Then you have an *Alien!*

Matthew Ward-Barber (10) Aston Rowant School

PENGUINS

Penguins like eating fish,
that's their only dish,
Penguins are my favourite
animals, so please don't
hurt the mammals.
Penguins like eating fish.

Philip Hodge (9) Aston Rowant School

IF I WERE A QUEEN OF ENGLAND

If I was Queen of England
I would give food for beggars to eat,
and children a whole street.
Everybody has then a house
and nobody has to look like a mouse.

If I was Queen of England
I would close all the schools
and nobody has to sit on the cold stools.
Everybody can play the whole day,
and nobody has to go their own way.

Aneke Orth (10) Aston Rowant School

RECIPE FOR A WOLF

Take a frying pan
Throw in claws and fangs
Fry it for a minute and leave it to cool
Cut an inch of fluff
Boil in a pot
But don't forget a cold wet nose and blood red eyes
Get the claws and fangs
Mix them in the pot
Then sprinkle chalk and coal
For a wonderful colour
Freeze for a day
Then you will have a wolf.

Teresa Garratty (10) Aston Rowant School

LEAF PICNIC

I was sweeping up the leaves today,
about to put them in the bin.,
But then I thought and said, 'I won't,
They'll do nicely for a caterpillar's dinner.'

Steven Cook (10) Aston Rowant School

CATS

Cats sleep under chairs.
Cats sleep anywhere.
Cats sleep on beds.
Cats sleep snoring heads.

Cats sleep on settees.
Cats sleep on your knees.
Cats sleep with no sound.
Cats sleep all around.

Johnny Boulton (10) Aston Rowant School

ON THE SEA FRONT

The rough sea crashes
Against the rocks
I stand on the flat hard
Limestone as the sea breeze
Brushes through my hair
The water is so cold as it
Splashes over my toes.

Roxanne Smith (10) Aston Rowant School

THE BIG TREE

This tree is so big and old
You could tell stories about it that have never been told
This tree has got leaves everywhere
You could never trim it bare
Its bark is dark and very moist
And if I had one choice
I would have this tree for myself
Because this tree is so big and old.

Gemma Walker (10) Aston Rowant School

AN 'I AM' POEM

I am tall and slim
I can be sharp or blunt
keep turning me and I will
shrink
My coat can be all different
colours
But my stem will always be
grey.

      Who am I?

Jenna Green (9) Aston Rowant School

HISS THE SNAKE

Hiss the snake is my name
Catching mice is my game
I slip and slide all day long,
A hiss and a spit and I am gone.

Hannah Allworth (8) Aston Rowant School

MY CAT

I have a cat called Daisy
Who is very, very lazy.
All she does is eat and sleep
And catches shrews and moles to eat.

She sleeps on my bed at night
And gives me a terrible fright
When she jumps on my bed and licks my face
Before going out to hunt mice.

Holly Jones (8) Aston Rowant School

DANCING DAFFODILS

Dancing daffodils in the sun
A new morning has just begun,
Swaying tulips to and fro
We like to see them grow and grow.

Craig Merrell (9) Aston Rowant School

POLLUTION

Stop! Pollution! You have been told
I know that the world is old
But! We could make it live much longer
If we decide to make it stronger
By not putting rubbish on the floor
The world needs to be reborn!

     So Be
             Warned!

Stephanie Harwood (11) The Blake C E Primary School

NESSIE

In the lake of Loch Ness lived Nessie
A legend you say but it's not
I've seen her I have,
With my own blue eyes
She's big with a round nose and blue stripes.

She has a long curled tail
With a ball on the end
And a spot on the end of her eyelash.

She called to me 'Hi'
Then I woke up and I was surprised
To find it was all a dream.

Rachel Stace (11) The Blake C E Primary School

BASKET BALL

B ang goes the ball on the floor
A ttack isn't played with your hands
S wish goes the net
K emp is on a superb run
E veryone shouts
T ime out calls the coach

B oom goes the rim
A ll the crowd scream and shout
L egs are moving
L ong bodies run everywhere.

Michael Mullin (10) The Blake C E Primary School

RAINFORESTS

Rainforests are green
At night the forest is dark
It is dark and green

Rainforests are wet
At day the forests are wet
At night it is wet

Rainforests have birds
There are tropical birds and
Some birds fly at day

Rainforests have snakes
Rainforests have snakes that slither
Snakes slither about

Rainforests are damp
Rainforests have wet nature
Rainforests are moist

Rainforests have trees
Rainforests have lots of trees
The air is humid

Jenna King (9) The Blake C E Primary School

LITTER / TRASH

T urning rivers into junk, junk
R ain forests threatened by mankind
A ll the people have forgotten about the world
S hame all nature it's now in the past
H ave you cleaned up your atmosphere?

Ben Hockney (11) The Blake C E Primary School

LISTEN AND LEARN

Listen to the birds singing in the trees
listen to the animals all around me.
No, not in a few years' time,
unless we stop it now,
help the animals stop it now.

pollution in the river
pollution in the air,
pollution from the cars,
pollution everywhere,
killing helpless animals everywhere.

Daniel O'Dell (11) The Blake C E Primary School

SUMMER TIME IS BACK

Insects crawling all around
Leaves blowing across the ground
Bees buzzing in the trees
Fish swimming in the sea

Worms wriggling in the ground
Roses and Fox gloves to be found
Birds flying all around
Juicy black berries to be found

Trees blowing in the breeze
Beavers gnawing at the trees
Pollen falling from the bees
Summer time is back!

Tiffany Wishart (9) The Blake C E Primary School

SUMMERTIME

Trees trees blowing in the breeze
Birds flying overhead
Bees bees buzzing around
Trees swaying in the breeze
Worms wriggling around underground
Fish swimming in the cool river
Moles popping
Up and down from the ground.

Stacey Forward (10) The Blake C E Primary School

LITTER

Litter is everywhere
Litter makes me feel sad
Litter is in pond and streams
Litter is bad
Litter is pollution
Litter makes us ill
Litter makes me angry
        but people litter still.

Nathaniel Miles (10) The Blake C E Primary School

ANIMALS

A parrot is very pretty because
of all their lovely colours like
red, blue, green and yellow
I think they are nice.

Tigers are vicious and not very
nice but when they have been
trained they are really very nice.

Monkeys are nice
they swing back and forth
all day and night.

Kayleigh Provins (9) Caldecott Primary School

MY PETS

My little puppy
he is very fluffy
He plays all day
All he does is lay in the bay.

My little kittens
they play with my mittens
All they do is chase mice
but they're still very nice.

My goldfish
she eats off a dish
They like bishops
so I call my fish, Fishops.

My little rabbit
runs round the garden all day
All he likes is fun and play.

Lauren Rossiter (9) Caldecott Primary School

COUGH, SNIFF, SNEEZE!

I cough at my auntie's
I sniff at my gran's
I sneeze at my uncle's
I don't use my hands!

When I cough at my auntie's
She screams and she shouts
But it's that flippin' great ciggy,
She breathes in and out.

When I sniff at my granny's
She shouts 'Blow your nose'
But I think it's her perfume
'*La Bella, La Rose*'.

When I sneeze at my uncle's
He bellows and shouts,
But it's his dog I'm allergic to,
(Bloomin' great lout!)

Last night I nicked all aunt's ciggies,
And took my uncle's dog,
I shoved him in the pantry,
And flushed the ciggies down the bog!

And what with granny's perfume?
I threw it down the drain,
I hope I never see these things,
Ever, ever again.

Laura Oultram (11) Caldecott Primary School

ANDROID ATTACK

Androids came down from Andromeda
One day called Wednesday 1,
From the dreaded planet Z,
Like bullets from a gun.

They stirred up all the chaos
By blowing up London,
They only thought it was
A little bit of fun.

'Give the Android Life,
Amen, Amen, Amen,'
Was one of the ghastly prayers
From the android den.

They turned all of the GADJET spies
Into androids now,
Really why they did this,
Is wondered more than how.

This dreaded attack of course,
Was more like world war 3,
Something *they* won't have to do
Is pay the dreaded fee.

Androids at the moment
Are just trying to kill,
Someone called the Savage Cat . . .
And they really will.

Graham Morris (9) Caldecott Primary School

MY KITTEN

My kitten is fluffy
she is white as snow
her name is Misty her
eyes are green.

My little kittens play
with my mittens
all they do is chase
mice but still they're nice.

My kitten plays night and day
all she does is play.

She cuddles up by the fire
while I'm knitting with my wool
She gives me a cuddle and
a moan.

I've got a picture of her hanging
on the wall, but it doesn't
look like her at all.

Emily Constance (9) Caldecott Primary School

EAGLE

Swishing swooping across the sky is an eagle
flying high.
On the mountain over there is that bird of prey
Catching its food for its dinner again.
It flies to the river to hunt for its fish
It opens its claws to catch it. It's eating
It now, poor fish.

Lucy Bough (9) Caldecott Primary School

FOXES

In the deep dark woodland foxes running
across the woodland floor.
Squirrel climbing tree to tree and foxes anxiously
trying to catch its prey.
Creeping silently through the green with his belly low
and his eyes yellow.
He has a fearsome grin and sharp teeth and
enormous paws and two inch claws and leaps to catch
his prey.

Katherine Newbold (10) Caldecott Primary School

THE EAGLE

There's an eagle near the mountain flying around,
It's looking for something on the ground,
I could watch it all day long,
That bird looks so strong.

The eyes on it look great,
I think it's looking for its bait,
It's seen something I think,
The eagle's tummy looks rather pink.

No wait, it's red, he's bleeding,
Stop that eagle, he's leaving,
We drove him from his habitat to the vet,
Who says he was probably caught in a net?

The vet looked after him for us,
On the way home we took the bus,
I hoped that bird was okay,
'The eagle's better now' I heard the vet in my mind say.

Laura Wells (11) Caldecott Primary School

TOUCANS

Toucans hop from tree to tree.
One spots a juicy berry
It tosses it into the air and then
catches it again.
Soon the toucan wants to rest
he puts his bill on to his chest.
Now the jungle is quiet again
except the sound of the jungle rain.

Emily Warder (10) Caldecott Primary School

MY DIFFERENT PETS

I have a pet pig who wears a wig
He lives in a sty
And eats mashed potato pie
People think he's weird and ugly
But who cares what they think
I think he's lovely
My pet pig
      called Fig

My pet frog lives in a bog
And sleeps like a log
And is called Trog
He plays for hours and hours
My pet frog
      called Trog

My pig with a wig
My frog in a bog
What a collection I have got!

Natalie Kathryn Allred (11) Caldecott Primary School

I COULD BE LIKE LEMON DROPS

I could be like lemon drops, underneath the bottle tops,
In the bottle dry and clean, in the bottle to be seen. In the
bottle the sun is there, in a bottle in a lair. In the bottle
right as rain, in the bottle outside in the rain. Inside outside of
the shop, being picked by kids a lot. All my family have disappeared,
they've been picked by children near. Soon it's me, in a bag,
along with friends to another land.

Alison Trotman (10) Caldecott Primary School

MESSING ABOUT

In my shed
I have a bed
which is a mess
I jump on my bed
without any fuss
my mum doesn't mind
if I jump so high
In my shed there's a hole
and when it rains
it floods my shed
But I don't care
It's still my shed
And when it's wet
I'm soaked to death
But it doesn't matter
It's only my shed.

Melissa Head (10) Caldecott Primary School

BIRDS

Birds swoop like a glider in the sky
They twist like a kite
They chirp their little melodies
Birds in the garden digging for worms
like a shovel digging for gold.

Kimberley Furze (10) Caldecott Primary School

THE SHIVERING STARS

The moonlight shines
Over me,
So when I go out
In the darkness of the night
And I can see
My way back home.

The stars shiver in the sky
I point to one and say
There is the Great Bear
Shivering and shining
Up there.

The children are playing
In the sun light
And singing
I look at the sun
And it smiles at me.

Alice Warder (7) Caldecott Primary School

TIGERS

In the deep dark jungle a tiger's roar
Echoes across the jungle floor
Monkeys leap from tree to tree
Chattering anxiously *(not me, not me!)*
Creeping silently through the green
Can you guess what he has seen?
With his belly low and his eyes aglow
He has a fearsome grin with sharp teeth in
and enormous paws with six inch claws.
He leaps and devours his prey.

Lucy Smith (10) Caldecott Primary School

THE BIRD AND THE WORM

I'm a bird
In a playground
Watching children play,
I can see a juicy worm,
Next up for today.

I'm a worm
On the ground
Wriggling around,
Suddenly a big black bird,
Scooped me off the ground.

Michael McCormack (11) Caldecott Primary School

MY BUBBLE BATH

My bath in bubbles
Bubbles in your teeth
Bubbles in your hair
Bubbles are everywhere.

I'll get a nail
and I'll pop them
till they drop
pop pop pop.

Simonne Blair (10) Caldecott Primary School

IN THE PARK

In the park, I play chase
With all my friends and mates,
I run at a very good pace,
So they can't catch me!

I hid beside the tree
And knelt on one knee
To have a rest, I think
My friends are the
        Best!

Cheryl Harris (11) Caldecott Primary School

I'M A MONSTER

I'm a green monster with 20 eyes
I have one wing
But I cannot sing
But I cannot sing
But I can go ping
Or ring a ding ding.

I'm not that big,
But I can dig
Or eat a fig like a pig
I can see the fig 20 times
And I like *Me!*

Anthony Gleeson (11) Caldecott Primary School

RIVERS

I hear the river splashing
past
crashing rocks water going
fast
fishes swimming in and
out ducks going quack quack
quack
I smell the pollution
I feel the slimy reeds.

Chris Webb (8) Caldecott Primary School

PEOPLE IN THE PLAYGROUND

People in the playground playing all day,
People in the playground work and play,
People in the playground have lots of fun
                                    and sit in the sun,
People in the playground eating their lunch,
People in the playground having a munch,
People in the playground climb the trees,
People in the playground playing hide and seek.

Donna Collins (9) Caldecott Primary School

POLAR BEAR

The polar bear is white so is snow,
The polar bear is camouflaged in the snow,
It eats fish and swims in the cold seas;
The polar bear goes swimming to catch his food.
Yum, it's eating the cold fish in the freezing cold ocean.
The Antarctic is a very cold place with a lot of snow.
It is all white.
As white as can be.

Liam Bramall (10) Caldecott Primary School

Y

I wish I could fly
With the letter (Y)
High up in the sky
Wishing and waving
With the letter (Y).

Jenna Brown (11) Caldecott Primary School

KARATE TOURNAMENT

Slowly walk up
quaking jaw
painful stitch
muscles grinding
loud shout
lurch forward
feeling sick
dry throat
painful stitch
small mistake
loud shout
lurch forward
slowly walk down
hope I've passed
Sensei comes to tell me if I've passed
I've passed!
loud cheer from the crowd
it's *amazing!*

Jamie M White (11) Edward Feild CP School

INVENTING

I've already designed three things.
I've told my friends at school.
They burst out in laughter.
They think I'm a fool.
When I get older I'll be famous.
I'll have lots of dosh and cash
They won't think I'm silly then.
I won't waste any trash.

Tim Archard (8) Edward Feild CP School

DISNEY WEEK

What a week that was
the week we went to Disney.
Mickey, Minnie all were there
with all the fun of the fair to share.
Peter Pan's ride up in the stars
up and down nearly to Mars.
The pirate's ride all creepy and dark
underground where the treasures are.
The runaway train all blowy and fast,
ducking and diving in tunnels all dark.
Mary Poppins she was there,
with her umbrella up high in the air.
That was the best week ever that was.
The week we went to Disney.

Laura Pollard (8) Edward Feild CP School

LEAVE IT

Among the grass a daisy stood
Hiding in the sunny wood

I want to pick it
and lots more like it
to make a chain with it.

Should I or should I not?

I think I'll leave the wood
and the daisy.

I feel very hot!

Hannah Pearce (8) Edward Feild CP School

MY TREASURE

I have some letters
    special to me

I keep them safe
    as could be

I keep them under
    my pillow at night

I read them
    in the morning light

I have some letters
    special to me

I keep them safe
    as could be

They're from my nannie
    who lives far from me.

Holly Lambourne (9) Edward Feild CP School

TO MY MOTHER

If I were you
And you were me
You would see
How ill I am.
You would let
Me stay off school
If I were you
And you were me.

Gareth Siret (9) Edward Feild CP School

ON THE WILD SIDE

Nearly every minute a baby is born,
Lion cubs, hippos and fawns.
Out on the *wild side*, up they grow,
With no impatience, oh so slow.
Bigger and bigger and bigger they get,
Living life being nobody's pet.

Many times there's men with guns,
Spoiling their day and making them run,
Bang, bang, bang, now they're dead,
Hyenas and vultures will soon be fed.
Ripping them from limb to limb,
In the moonlight, oh so dim.

I suppose nearly all animals in the wild kill,
And they eat their prey to get their fill.
Fishes, animals and birds,
Go around in flocks and herds.
All of them have to kill to eat,
Using other creatures for their meat.

Every animal will fall in love,
Tigers, sharks, snakes and doves,
And they will go on an animal date,
Then that night they will mate.
They will find their special one,
Have their babies, and some fun.

Joanne Eagle (10) Edward Feild CP School

FLOWERS

Since roses are red
they make me feel like bed
Since bluebells are blue
they make me feel like I've got the flu
Since snowdrops are white
they make me feel very bright.

Camille Dunkley (9) Edward Feild CP School

MY DOLLY

I had a dolly very innocent
in everything she was meanest.
One day we went for a walk
and she drank all my coke.
I was very cross she thinks
she is the boss.
We had a fight then I used
her as knife.

Zehra Chudry (8) Edward Feild CP School

MARY MARIGOLD

Mary Marigold is very pretty
She grows up very high
She lives in a golden city
With a lovely turquoise sky.

Kate Broadbent (9) Edward Feild CP School

RATTLING RAIN

The rain comes
rattling dripping
rattle rattle clickety clunk
pitter patter drip drip
tiss tiss tiss tiss
tiss tiss tiss tiss tiss
clitter clang
rain against the windows
rain making little puddles
soon a *massive flood*
crashing across the city.

The sun needs a drink
zip zip through a straw
making the flood die
more and more
quick quicker
children in the street
the rain's gone gone gone.

Jade Laforest (9) Edward Feild CP School

MY SISTER'S A PAIN IN THE NECK

She's always following me around
She always takes over when my friend
comes to call
She always wants what I've got
She's always there when I need a friend
But my sister's a pain in the neck.

Carima Ghani (8) Edward Feild CP School

THE EURO ANIMAL

An animal came to our house one day
and greeted us in every way
Buenos Dias, Bonjour, Guten Tag, Hello
As it wagged its tail to and fro.

I offered it a plate of Sauerkraut
But it choked and quickly spat it out
Roast Beef, frogs' legs and calamari did the trick
For which I got a grateful lick.

It drank beer, Sangria and red wine
All of which by me was fine
Until it started dancing the Flamenco
Now it really was time for it to go!

Its bright blue fur I gently stroked
Only to find my feet were soaked
It had spent a penny, or rather a Euro
Its chances of staying now were zero.

Auf wiedersehen, Arriverderchi, Au revoir, Goodbye
It sloped away with a painful sigh.
And then I noticed as it fled
A crown of golden stars around its head.

Ali Hakimi (11) Edward Feild CP School

MUM GETS MAD

I needed to iron my dress.
But I'm not allowed
to use the iron on my own.
I got the iron out,
put it on the floor
and started ironing
my foot nudged the lead
which made the iron fall . . .
I burnt a big hole in the carpet.
I thought 'Oops! I'm in trouble
Big trouble
I'll be grounded till I die.'

S l o w l y

    U p

        T h e

            S t a i r s

I wake up my mum, she said loudly
*'What do you mean
A hole in the carpet'*
I think, 'She's going to kill me . . .'

Lauren Davis (9) Edward Feild CP School

RELIEVED

Standing there behind the block
feeling tense and nervous
yet feeling determined and ready to go
then all of a sudden the whistle blows
and I'm down on hands and feet
the whistle goes again
I'm in the racing position
then there's silence
the gun goes.
I push off the block with all my might
A minute later I'm racing down the pool
legs kicking hard and arms pulling me downwards
I'm five metres away from the turn
I'm counting in to the turn 1 2 3 4 and
turn, my arm pulling me round,
I turn the right way then push off
I glide for a while then come to the surface
do three strokes then breathe, goggles
begin to fill with water, getting tired now
half-way there now getting excited
wondering what place I'm in, hoping
it's first. I'm five metres away form the end
kicking and pulling faster now I'm one stroke
away from the end I make a good finish
I look round to see who else has finished
As I look they finish. Yes, I came *first*.
I am feeling breathless but *relieved!*

Hayley Carter (10) Edward Feild CP School

THE VENOMOUS EMPEROR

This is the story of the venomous emperor;
    Who had an almighty and quite fiery temper.
Many were beheaded, because of his great rage;
    That's why many houses were, protected by a cage.

Now he woke up one fine morning, the sun was in the sky.
    All the lovely birds were singing, and a traitor was to die.
He set about his business as he sat on his great throne;
    He slaughtered half a field of sheep and laughed,
                     'I am baaad to the bone!'
He shot his secretary, and he fired the grim reaper;
    And when he stole a thousand yuan he cackled,
                     'Now life'll be cheaper!'
But on this day, this lovely day, goodness would be brought;
    To the great empire that destruction had long sought.
A ninja with a golden sword was hiding in a curtain;
    The evil emperor's destruction was obviously certain.
The ninja screeched, and then he jumped up in the air;
    He threw a pair of shurikens that sliced in half a chair.
The emperor was quite impressed but did not know his fate;
    Or that soon his title would become very *late*.
The ninja leapt across the room, a nunchuck in each hand;
    The emperor just watched the ninja come to a land.

The ninja's golden sword lashed out!
Which the emperor tried to avoid . . .
But he was sliced quite clean in half;
And all were overjoyed!

Now the emperor was dead, the ninja took the throne,
    To make sure peace and goodness rule, and he was to be
                                      well-known.
His name was *Elvis* . . .

David Stanmore (11) Edward Feild CP School

THE WATERFALL

The water crashes down
and bounces off rocks
splash splash it
lands in the
flowing
river.

Jodie Evans (9) Freeland CE Primary School

CRASHING ROCKS

Down comes the water
And crashes on the rocks,
Thinking of the mighty sea
It's always like the locks.

Down comes the water,
And crashes on the stream,
The willow trees dangle
In the water of the bream.

Claire Watson (8) Freeland CE Primary School

JUMP

I watch the clear water in the
swimming pool.
As clear as clear can be.
'The water must be cold' I say.
So what do I do?
I jump in!

Charlotte E Barrow (8) Freeland CE Primary School

WATERFALLS

Waterfalls are really tough.
Waterfalls can be rough.
You can surf on a waterfall,
But only the ones that are very small.
Frogs float on lilies on a waterfall,
But the problem is they always
Seem to fall.

Lorna Moir (8) Freeland CE Primary School

THE LEOPARD GECKO IN WATER

Lizard.
Lies in water
Water rushes over him
and under him.
His skin gets slimy
and water gets in his
eyes.
His tail splashes
in the water.

Mark Crocker (8) Freeland CE Primary School

THE SEA

The sea crashes against the rocks,
animals hide.
The thunder crashes, rain pours down
and lands on the ocean floor.

Jamie Lawes (8) Freeland CE Primary School

SEA

Water rushing free makes me feel so free and when
it makes me feel free I can dive in the sea but
I must be careful of the jaws.

Thomas McNeil (8) Freeland CE Primary School

WATER

The water comes out of the wall
The water comes out of the sky
The water comes out of the puddles
and the water goes down the drainpipes.

Sebastian Delaisse (9) Freeland CE Primary School

THEME OF WATER

The horrible tidal wave,
When it comes people pray to be saved.
It washes everything away,
So you would not like to stay,
In a horrible tidal wave.

One day I went to a pool,
Oh, it was lovely and cool,
I decided to dive,
It splashed onto a beehive,
So the bees came out and were angry.

Jamie Barlow (8) Freeland CE Primary School

WATER

Sometimes I go down to the river with
my dad and we see the water
rushing at the rocks and we
step in the water.
The river rushing against your feet and
rolling back. When our feet
were out, the water made its way
through.

Jade Berry (8) Freeland CE Primary School

WATERFALLS

Down comes the water and
crashes on the rocks.
It goes so fast that it runs into an
old cardboard box.
The water crashes on the sides and
splashes everywhere!

Rebecca Leggett (8) Freeland CE Primary School

LET WATER COME

Water! Water! I'm scared of water.
Go, go, go away water! I hate water!
Under water, sharp jaws, sharks' teeth
Bite, jellyfish sting your legs.
I hate water!

Robert Atherton (9) Freeland CE Primary School

WATERFALLS

Waterfalls are great fun
It's really hot under the sun.
It's really fun to go under,
It's really not fun with rain and thunder.
It's mostly really good,
If it's raining I would wear a coat
with a hood.
Imagine if you went behind the waterfall
and saw a door, if you open the door
it might lead to a concrete floor.

Lucie Watson (8) Freeland CE Primary School

FANTASY POOL

As the moonlight,
Shone on the
Warm silvery pool,
The water made
Tiny ripples which
Turned into
Little waves.
As the artistic picture
Carried on going,
The music got louder
And louder.

Audur Alexandersdottir (9) Freeland CE Primary School

LOST AND ALONE

Once there was a little puppy .
Its fur was brown and white,
its nose was pink and dimpled
and his eyes were filled with fright.
Then an old lady came and picked him up.
'How nice' she said, 'what a sweet little pup!'
She took him home and sat him by the fire
and his eyes gave a twinkle like a sparkling sapphire.
She named him Patch because of his spot,
and he jumped on her lap where it was cosy and hot.
The old lady said 'What a shame!'
when in through the door he came.
Her cat Ashley had come with big yellow eyes
and gave Patch a bit of a surprise.
Patch thought he would take a nap
when Ashley saw him sitting on her lap.
His fur stood up, his tail was like a loo brush.
He ran at Patch with one big rush.
He jumped at Patch with one big leap.
Patch thought he would make his retreat.
He jumped through the window and Ashley through the door
'He'll never come back,' she said 'for sure.'
But the old lady was strong and bold
and took Ashley to market where he was sold.
Patch ran and ran, day and night,
and only stopped when it was light.
Patch fell over a stone and fell in a ditch,
then he heard a noise like a cackling witch.
A man jumped out with a big net
and said 'Where's that dog I'm trying to get?'
He found Patch and put him in a lorry
with two other dogs and a dog named Polly.

He was taken to the pound and his eyes were filled with tears.
He stayed at the pound for years and years.
Then the old lady came 'Patch,' she said, 'what a crime
wait till everyone hears you've been here all this time.'
No more scum on fur for Patch because she's a *mum!*

Eleanor Atherton (8) Freeland CE Primary School

LAZY LIZARD

I'm a lazy old lizard
Who lives at the zoo
And catches the flies
And swallows them too.

Richard Wood (8) Freeland CE Primary School

WATERFALLS

Waterfalls
are such a sight to see
watching when the water gushes
free,
curving round the rocks as we see
waterfalls make me so
      happy!

Kate Wylie (8) Freeland CE Primary School

REFLECTION

As I walk along the river
My reflection follows me so
I sit on the bank and put my
hand in and it ripples. I suddenly
disappear into thin air

Rebecca Mutlow (9) Freeland CE Primary School

ACROSTIC

W aiting for water all day long.
A iming at the target not at you.
T ouching all the daffodils but not touching you
E vaporating water out of all the flowers
R ain, rain the plants go dry, next year they will die.

Faye Bunting (9) Freeland CE Primary School

THE OLD MAN OF THE SEA

The old man of the sea
is always there so when you're
at sea always beware.
He controls the waves
he controls the lightning
he makes the sea fierce he
makes the sea frightening.
Treat the sea with respect and
he will calm down
but the old man of the sea
is never to be found . . .

Ian Moore (8) Freeland CE Primary School

THE PEBBLE

First I was sitting on the beach with
the other pebbles,
Then a boy kicked me I landed at
the bottom of the sea.
All I do is watch fish and sharks
swim by.
Oh no! I'm being washed away.
I'm being washed past all the fish I wish
I wish I was back on the beach.
I nearly got squashed by an anchor from
an old tanker.
Now a wave has shot me out of the
sea landing with a splash.
Sinking down, getting darker, clank.

Jamie Warner (9) Glory Farm School

ANCHOR

Overboard goes the anchor, I am on the waves
going to the bottom, the rope snaps and now
I'm getting further and further away from the old
ship itself. I got to the beach, I laid
there for years and years.
Still got the memory of the old ship
then human people came up to me and
lifted me up, took pieces of me
and dropped me down to die in peace.

Joshua Thomson (10) Glory Farm School

THE CANDLE

I am waiting on the floor.
I hope I am not burnt.
Only a little candle
That is all I am I will never be free.
Here comes that human again and
                he's got some matches.
Oh no, I'm going to be burnt.
It's been lit, I'm going to die.
I'm burning, I am no more.

Gary Venters (10) Glory Farm School

THE DEAD PAIR OF SHOES

We are attached by a lace
and we can run in a race,

We are the kings of your feet,
We try to keep them tidy and neat,
And when they aren't washed too well,
They really have a whiff, a kind of smell.

And when we get ripped, torn
And we die,
There is a sudden wetness
When you start to cry.
We get thrown and, we stay in the bin,
and how come that other pair you've got,
Is your next of kin?

Martin Winstone (10) Glory Farm School

MY OLD CLOCK

I am standing on the dusty shelf
Tick tock tick tock.
Waiting for someone to come to see what's the time.
Tick tock tick tock.
Dust is all over my dry nose
am sneezing, am sneezing.
Tick tock tick tock.
Am alone in this old dark wet house in this old dark, smelly room.
There's no-one to clean me.
Tick tock oh no! The batteries have stopped.

Naomi Calderon (10) Glory Farm School

A BOOK

I am a book on the book shelf.
I will tell you a bit about myself,
I'm a book called Treasure Island,
I am colourful and brand new,
My neighbour has been covered in glue.
He told me to watch out for Daniel Roo,
He was the one who covered him in glue,
Daniel Roo is coming over here
He is getting very near.
He has picked me up
Got some glue
Now I am covered in glue too.

Lyndon Davis (10) Glory Farm School

PEBBLE

I am a pebble,
I live on the bottom of the river,
As I crash against the bank of the river,
I feel my sides wasting away.

As I speak to my friends
I can feel the river getting faster and faster,
Telling my friend about the way I feel.

I feel rotten,
I feel when this journey ends, I will have *vanished,*
Broken into tiny pieces.

The water is getting slower and slower,
The river is getting wider,
I wonder what's happening.
At last I have all the space in the world.

Kashia E Adams (10) Glory Farm School

THE ELEPHANT

It was pain and agony when
they tried to take my tusks.
I could see the dagger coming
closer and closer. Then it all went
blank, but I could still hear the
man saying 'This is a good tusk.'
Then I could not hear or see because
I was going, going, *gone!*

Danielle Prpa (10) Glory Farm School

TREE

I am a tree in the woods all lonely,
wanting someone to come and chop me down
and be a book so people can read me and
enjoy my pictures.

I don't care what book I am as long as
they enjoy me.
I would love to be a blue shiny book with
a gold rim.

Daniel Hewer (10) Glory Farm School

THE OLD PAIR OF KEYS

Being put into the keyholes,
Turning around and around
Being taken out of the keyhole
Going back into the dark purse
The button is doing up
In here for the rest of the day
Being given to someone else
Who is it?
Where are they going?
There, back in a week
I'm given back
Hooray!
I'm so pleased to be given back
But in I go
Back in the boring dark purse
Oh no, the purse is dropped
I'm stuck in the purse forever.

Claire Ford (9) Glory Farm School

WONDERFUL RUGBY

That tackle,
That kick,
The skill in that pass,
Have all been seen in Rugby's wonderful past.

The ruck
The maul
The line-out jumping tall
Have all been seen in Rugby's wonderful past.

Andrew Morris (10) Glory Farm School

THE OLD SHOES

I am a pair of old shoes.
I'm really dirty.
Really need to be cleaned.
No-one to talk to.
Here comes that cleaning brush,
He's cleaning me too.
I am really shiny too.
Looking really new.
Somebody is wearing me.
It feels like a treat.
Going to a big fun fair.
Getting on a ride.
I will be home very soon.
Nearly fast asleep.
Hope I'm not used for a while.

Donna Butler (9) Glory Farm School

THE OLD ARMCHAIR

I'm sitting all on my own,
In a dark spooky house,
In a dark scary room,
Waiting for someone to sit on me,
I'm all ripped and tattered,
It's so cold and damp in here,
Hang on I hear loud steady footsteps
Oh no! It's the water dripping,
I guess no-one will sit on me,
Because I'm still sitting on my own.

Tina Matthews (10) Glory Farm School

THE PEBBLE

I'm waiting on the sandy, wet beach.
For somebody to pick me up and admire me,
Take me home where I'll be lovely and hot,
Just dreams,
But wait, here comes someone now.
'Ouch!' That hurt he kicked me into the sea,
'Help me! Help me! Help, I'm drowning!'

Now I've been picked up. Hooray!
Warmth, I can feel it now.
'Oh no!' I'm being skimmed. 'Help!'

Wesley Lewis (10) Glory Farm School

BOOK

I'm sitting on the shelf watching people grow up.
People haven't stirred me for over ten years.
I'm just sitting here.
I watch children play and laugh.
Life goes on and on.
I have chats with the other books.
One day I was moved away.
Away from my friends.
I was put on the table.
I was opened and my secrets floated out
I was ruined
They threw me out.

Lauren Spencer (9) Glory Farm School

FOOTSTEPS

On a dark cold night
Shadows appearing everywhere
Rats surrounding you from their
gloomy holes
Not a sound but suddenly a cry came from
nowhere 'Attack!' all the guards woke up from
snoozing.
Rats running back in their holes
Hearing footsteps people running in all
directions.
Sounds of guns, blood everywhere
People dying, dying, dying, *dead!*

Danielle Reading (10) Glory Farm School

AN OLD CAR'S STORY

Here I am rusting on my own old scrap heap
Longing for the day when I will come to an end
I used to be new, glittering under the showroom lights
The chrome grating at my front was shining
My owner took great care of me, polishing me and cleaning
Until this fancy blue sports car came
He robbed me of my pride and joy
I was sold to another owner to be a test car for learners,
I bumped into cones and flew over bumps,
My leather seats were ripped and I started rusting
They looked at me and said 'No, no!'
I was sold to the scrapman, and *now* I'm all alone.

Marc Abbey (10) Glory Farm School

MY HAIRBRUSH

My hairbrush looks really gross
It's got lots of little pink heads
Stuck on purple pins.
Underneath the pins is a
Cushion of air
And when I put my finger
Between the pins and push
The pins surround my finger.

My hairbrush may look gross
But it feels nice in my hair.
And is very useful in the morning
When my hair is trying to touch
The ceiling.

Daniel Wood (10) Glory Farm School

THE PENCIL STRIKES AGAIN

I am in my jar
Waiting to be used
Here come the people
They choose Kashia
Nobody is here
I am all alone
In a quite big jar
Wait here a minute
Here comes somebody
I jump up and down
Try to attract them
He goes right past me
No-one likes me
I am just so sad
The jar is my friend
It is boring here
All my friends have gone
No-one to talk to,
It's home-time again.

Stacey Moody (9) Glory Farm School

THE RAINDROPS

I see the raindrops
splashing on the floor
falling on the treetops
knocking at the door
dancing on the tiles
making big puddles
falling for miles
and getting me in muddles.

Joanna Wilkinson (9) Glory Farm School

POEM

I am an ordinary piece of A4 paper
I'm sitting here playing *I spy with my little eye.*
Suddenly someone picks me up.
They're folding me up into an unconventional shape.
Now he's throwing me, *wheeeeeee*
I'm swooping through the air . . . Oh no!
My sharp bit has landed on the teacher's nose.
'Ow' I said 'that hurt'. He's ripping me up.
'Yuck!' He's thrown me into the bin and I've landed
on a soggy banana.
This is ghastly.

Sam Burnand (9) Glory Farm School

WHAT AM I?

I am scaly,
I live in the salty sea,
I glide on my side,
I come in all colours,
I come in all sizes,
I eat seaweed,
I can blow bubbles,
I am tasty with chips,
I can dive in the sea,
I may be eaten by a whale,
What am I?

I am a fish.

Gemma Tomalin (8) Kingham CP School

WEATHER RECIPE

To make sunset:
Ingredients:
2 eggs
A bowl
A whisk
2 Oranges
2 Apricots
Fridge

Take 2 eggs
Remove the yolk and put it in a bowl,
Mix together until yellow and soft.
Squeeze 2 oranges to remove the juice.
Add 25 drops of juice to the mixture.
Put in the fridge for 6 minutes then
throw up into the sky.
Remove when dark.

Scarlette Matthews (8) Kingham CP School

SUNSHINE

Hot and shiny
The sun comes down
Beating to keep me warm.
The sun is blazing down on me.
Big orange and yellow surrounds me.

Sophia Alidina (8) Kingham CP School

THUNDER STORM

Crash!
Bang!
Wallop!
Hear the sound of thunder.
It makes me shiver in my socks,
as it tears up trees.
It's a danger - yet it is no stranger
Crash!
Bang!
Wallop!

Robert Shackelton (8) Kingham CP School

WHAT AM I?

I am smooth or rough, dotted or lined,
I am knobbly and hard,
And found washed up on a beach near the sea,
My colours are many, bright or dull,
What can I be?
    I am a shell.

I have armour, shining bright orange,
I eat just about anything before my eyes,
I am rough and bumpy,
I am snappy and hard,
What am I?
    I am a crab.

Alice Bagnall (8) Kingham CP School

FOG

Fog - fluffy and white.
Swirling around you.
People look like shadows - so blurry cars
In a haze look like alien figures.
Damp and drizzly people hurrying home
to a nice, gold, hot fire.
Fog never ending in November
Please - go away fog!

Emily MacAvoy (8) Kingham CP School

WHAT AM I?

I am slimy, vicious and dangerous.
I am terrifying.
I have no transport except for my fin.
When I swim I dive into the water
which goes splash!
I have very big teeth and jaws.
My nickname is 'great white'.
I eat fish and humans and anything meaty.
I swim in the sea.
I glide through the water.
I swim with the boats.
I am smooth.
I am large.
I am blue often grey.
    What am I?
    I am a shark.

Morwenna Baylis (8) Kingham CP School

FOG

White and misty floating around all quiet and gloomy.
You never know where it ends - very spooky.
Just think someone could pop out and get you.
The mysterious thick clouds dreary and damp.
Flying around all thick and smooth,
The swirling smoke dull and dense.
The vapoury steam very blurry and spooky.
It makes you shiver in fright.
You could faint in all the white.

Edward Blake (8) Kingham CP School

THE SEA

The sea can be rough,
The sea can be wild,
The sea can be tough like a naughty child.

The sea can be wide,
The sea can be loud,
The sea can be big like a thunder cloud.

The sea can be angry,
The sea can be tough and roar,
The sea can be angry like a running boar.

The sea can be mighty,
The sea can be harmless,
The sea can be frisky like a bottle of whisky.

James Dawkes (8) Kingham CP School

THE SEA

The sea can be smooth,
The sea can be bubbly,
The sea can be tough,
Like a jumping bear.

The sea can be cracking,
The sea can be topping,
The sea can be magical,
Like a clapping bear.

The sea can be tough,
The sea can be rough,
The sea can be fluffy,
Like a jumping bear.

The sea can be cold,
The sea can be calm,
The sea can be foamy,
Like a glowing fish.

Mattea Cottle (8) Kingham CP School

HALLOWE'EN

This is the night when witches fly.
Half moon, heavy footsteps,
Orange pumpkins in my bed.
Shining like the little moon.
Twinkling stars in the sky.
This is the night when I can fly.
Witches wearing black hats,
Very floppy winged bats.

Hallowe'en - scary!

Emily Aldridge (8) Kingham CP School

FOG

Fog swirls, fog floats.
It's mysterious, I feel strange.
Fog is gloomy, full of frost.
It's cold, it can make you freeze.
It blots out sound.
It's so quiet.
It's only clear around you.
Fog is danger.
You can not see anything around you.
Fog is dense and has no colour.

Peter Fox (8) Kingham CP School

WHAT AM I?

I am large,
Black and white,
eat fish and seals,
have a fight.

I have a spout of water coming out of me,
I crash into the waves.
I have sharp teeth,
That can dig into anything I please.

I am silky,
I am smooth,
I am playful with my friends.
We dive into the salty sea,
What can I be?
    A whale.

Zoe McIntyre (8) Kingham CP School

THE SEA

The sea can be like a whale's tail in the air,
The sea can be cosy like a white unicorn.
The sea can be fun to play in and shallow.

The sea can be like a roaring lion.
The sea can be dangerous sometimes.
The sea can be a fierce tiger.
The sea can be like a wild animal.

The sea can be gentle.
The sea can be cold and calm.
The sea can be crystal clear.
The sea can be like a mirror.

The sea can be fished in,
The sea can be surfed on,
The sea can be seen from space.

Harry Shepherd (8) Kingham CP School

THE SEA

The sea can be comforting,
The sea can be harmless,
The sea can be calm,
like a white horse walking.

The sea can be playful,
The sea can be foamy,
The sea can be shiny,
like a playing dolphin.

The sea can be beautiful,
The sea can be deep,
The sea can be flat,
like a sleeping bat.

The sea can be rough,
The sea can be tough,
The sea can be noisy,
like a roaring lion.

Natalie Edwards (8) Kingham CP School

BEING LOVING

I'm loving when I'm happy,
I'm loving when I'm sad,
I'm loving when I'm mad,
But there's a feeling
When I'm not loving that's bad,
I'm loving when I'm mad
Because my Dad laughs
So I cuddle him!

Leanne Cadet (8) Mill Lane Primary School

DOGS

Dogs like fish
Dogs like water
Dogs chase cats
Dogs like sticks
Dogs can be any colour.

Marcus Hare (8) Mill Lane Primary School

FOX

Predator
Meat eater
Rabbit hunting
Cub kids
Black ears
Black button nose
Red fur
It is of course
        A fox.

Laura Joanne Stevenson (8) Mill Lane Primary School

SUMMER

Ants are coming out,
Ducklings are hatching,
Paddling pools are out.
Sun is shining brightly.
People eating ice-cream.
Flowers are opening.
Trees are getting leaves.
Buds are coming out as well.
Summer clothes are selling out.
Lollies are melting.
Hotels are full up.
Beaches fill up.
All the people that I know
Keep saying please don't go.

Laura Farhan (8) Millbrook CP School

SUMMER

Summer is coming, summer is here.
Summer is bright, summer is clear,
Summer is springtime, summer is fun,
Summer is hot, summer is the sun,
Summer is leaving, summer has gone,
Autumn is here. Autumn is long.

Jessica Dancy (8) Millbrook CP School

SUMMER

Summer is when you have the paddling pool out.
Summer is when flowers grow.
Summer is when baby lambs play.
Summer is hot and playful.
Summer is when you play outside.

Luke Talboys (8) Millbrook CP School

Y4

When you enter Y4 classroom,
You'll find some things
Which are not
Quite on the agenda.

Felicity laughing hysterically.

Nancy talking naughtily.

Sophie singing beautifully.

Robert gazing happily.

Mrs Gordon watching too!

Nancy Homewood : Our Lady's Convent Junior School, Abingdon

CAMPING

Let's go camping,
In the middle of a wood,
At night I hear the owls hoot,
I snuggle deep into my sleeping bag.

Let's go camping,
Down by the sea.
We can have a bar-b-que
And run and play on the beach.

Let's go camping,
In the farmer's field,
We will eat mushrooms for breakfast
Surrounded by nosy cows!

Let's go camping,
On the river bank
We can fish for our supper
And watch the boats go by.

Elizabeth Barclay (10) Our Lady's Convent Junior School, Abingdon

TULIPS

Tightly held together, the flower lets in no light,
The petals begin to unfold, showing off their scarlet beaks.
Crimson, rose and red but dipped in yellow paint.
For springtime is here!

Clustered in their crowds,
Gleaming in the springtime light
Satin petals formed, shining and smooth.
Tulips are out now!

Bees are buzzing all around, hungry for the pollen.
Look inside! The stamens stand up like insects' legs
In a star shaped pattern, six of them in all
Dancing round a maypole.

Now they droop and bend their heads
Falling to the ground
Petals broken, sadly
Another year has gone.

Jessica Edwards (9) Our Lady's Convent Junior School, Abingdon

SPRINGTIME!

Springtime is blooming all around
Daffodils and tulips shooting out of the ground
Blossom appearing on the trees
And slowly there is a gentle breeze.

Yellow and green are the colours of spring
With high in the sky an orangey thing
That orangey thing is a warming sun
Under whose beam we run and have fun.

Now the days are getting longer, you see
With a lot more hours of light for me
The next present will be the summer holiday
With a lot more time to play, play, play!

Christopher Byrne (9) Our Lady's Convent Junior School, Abingdon

BATTLE FOR VICTORY

The tension is tight not a soul in sight.
The bombers are coming in the dead of the night.
Enemy aircraft flying low.
Everyone hoping but they do not know.
The bomb is falling down and down.
But it has to land somewhere on the ground.
The King is praying.
The people are saying.
'Please bring our troops safely home.'
Black and ugly gas masks on.
There it is, the doodlebug bomb.
The soldiers carry plenty of fear
Then the siren sounds the all clear.

Lisa Brown (11) Rush Common School

AUSTRALIA

Australia is a land far away,
U can go there for a holiday!
Sometimes I dream of going there,
Today, tomorrow I don't care!
Relaxing by the big blue sea,
Adelaide is the place for me!
Living there would be such fun,
I think OZ is number one!
Australia is still a land far away!

Hayley Davies (11) Rush Common School

LOOK AT THE JUNGLES

What on earth has happened,
To all the parrots that chirped
They looked so beautiful
On their tree perch.

Now the jungles are just motorways
And all that runs through
Are whizzing coloured cars
Where the trees once grew.

Where are all the monkeys
That swing from tree to tree
Their cheeky little faces
That used to smile at me.

Now we have lost the jungles
Because of you and me
I miss all the animals
That used to play with me.

Every little flower
And every big tree
Had their own life
Which we took away carelessly.

Where on earth is it taking us?
At the end of the day
Why can't you just leave it
And go away.

Jenna Calcutt (11) Rush Common School

THIS WORLD

Animals in the world I love
like the dolphin and the sloth
even the snake and kangaroo.

There are endangered species
like the panda
even tigers too.

If we all looked after this world
there wouldn't be such things as endangered.
So do your best to look after this world
by picking up litter and stop cutting down trees
then this world would be happier
for you
me
and the animals.

Beccie Jones (10) Rush Common School

SPRING

The sun is out what a lovely day,
'I am happy' and that's what I love to say.
The birds are singing a delightful song,
It is just perfect not a bit wrong.
The pretty little flowers awake from
a deep sleep,
I think this flower I will keep,
A playful lamb in the field I see,
The person who loves the spring is me!

Sadie Ekers (9) St John's School, Banbury

THE CYCLOPS' LAMENT

Cyclops: They've all gone, and I am left alone,
　　　　　Sitting quietly on this rugged stone.
　　　　　My dark world stretches ahead of me,
　　　　　I pray to Poseidon, father let me see.

Chorus:　　He cries, he moans, he waves his hands,
　　　　　While Odysseus sails to different lands.
　　　　　He stamps his foot, the mountain shakes,
　　　　　He never sleeps, so never wakes.

Odysseus:　Cyclops you must be very thick,
　　　　　Because you did fall for my trick.
　　　　　You will never get me and my men,
　　　　　Because we are heading straight for our den.

Chorus:　　This is what Odysseus shouts,
　　　　　When he does jump about.
　　　　　His ship is sailing far away,
　　　　　All the way to Ithaca Bay.

Cyclops: I will get you, you stupid fool,
　　　　　You will be sucked up by the whirlpool.
　　　　　I am sure of this, it is definitely true,
　　　　　Otherwise the Scilla will go 'Boo!'

Chorus:　　Odysseus sails, Odysseus goes,
　　　　　And he will meet lots more foes.
　　　　　He will sail when the sun will shine,
　　　　　But he won't reach home for a long, long time.

Laurence Whyatt (10) St Joseph's RC Primary School, Carterton

THE MERMAID WHO WISHED FOR COMPANY

She sat on the rocks and stared at the sky.
Then she gave a little sad sigh,
and wished.
Her mouth was pulled right down.
Her tail had turned a dull brown.
She sat on the rocks and wished.
Her face was tear stained.
Her chest contained . . . a broken heart.
She sat on the rocks and wished,
She sat on the rocks and wished,
Wished for company.

Sarah Barton White (9) St Mary's Prep School, Henley

SOCKS

Odd socks, smelly socks, patterned socks,
Patterned socks go with frocks,
Odd ones and smelly ones don't,
I don't know why, they just won't,
Sitting at the bottom of the drawer waiting to be used.

But there are no shoes,
Needing to be filled,
Cause they're just chilled.

Smelly socks stink,
Like they've been worn by a mink
Odd socks are just a pain,
You look for them in vain,
Without any success,
For all you know they may belong to a princess!

Abbie Millward (9) St Mary's Prep School, Henley

ANIMALS OF THE EARTH

Eels slither, eels hide,
Eels swim round the riverside.
Dogs bark, dogs yelp,
Dogs are always there to help.
Pigs smell, pigs snort,
Pigs don't drink port.
Bees buzz, bees sting,
Bees never, ever sing.
Lions grow, lions scare,
Lions don't have underwear.
Ants bite, ants crawl,
Ants are hardly there at all.

Catherine Robinson (10) St Mary's Prep School, Henley

DRAGON

Dragon is fierce,
Dragon is mean,
She smells revolting,
She's sickly green.
She hides inside her dank lair,
No-one goes in, they couldn't bear,
To see and smell, to meet her, well!
To perish there, they wouldn't dare.
They wouldn't live to tell the tale,
They wouldn't speak and yes they'd fail,
To tell such a revolting tale!

Jessica Davis (10) St Nicolas School, Abingdon

SIMON'S MOUSE

Now Simon is a rather tallish fellow,
Skin all light, almost yellow.
And although I like him and his house,
I was not too fond of his pet mouse.

Once he scratched me with his claw,
And made me bellow my loudest roar,
Then he bit me with his teeth,
Oh and I forgot to tell you, his name is Keith.

I ran down the stairs and out the house,
Then came Simon, then the mouse.
We ran to the butcher Mrs Bush,
And she made the mouse into mush!

Richard Scott (10) St Nicolas School, Abingdon

THE MONSOON

Breeze at first,
Then the rain,
The howling, wet wind,
The warm refreshing rain,
Flooding over-flowing rivers,
Frightened people,
Fix umbrellas,
Out in the streets the children play,
In Goa on their holiday,
Now we definitely know,
The Monsoon is here.

Catherine Workman (10) St Nicolas School, Abingdon

HAPPINESS

Happiness is light pink,
And has a deep smell of roses,
It sounds like classical music,
It is as soft as petals,
It tastes like fresh, juicy strawberries,
When I'm with happiness I feel light and fluffy.

Simone Minal (10) St Nicolas School, Abingdon

RECIPE POEM

Take a tall goalkeeper
Sprinkle on some defenders
Then pour on some midfielders
Then add a pinch of forwards
Stir and leave for ninety minutes
Add two spoonfuls of skill
Then mix well.

William Drury (10) St Nicolas School, Abingdon

THE MONSOON

The rain pours down
Wet, windy, flooding the city.
Refreshing but frightening, whirling, splashing.
The sky is full of clouds,
Buckets of warm water thrown down,
The monsoon is here.

Richard Rawling (10) St Nicolas School, Abingdon

THE MONSOON

As warm as an English summer, as destructive as some anti-tank guns.
As rare as your birthday, as powerful as a hurricane,
Rivers turn into whirling death beds.
Roads turn into local swimming pools,
Fields turn into silent lakes,
Muddy grasses turn into swamps,
The rain dies down, the wind stops howling,
The monsoon carries onto the mountains,
Where more trouble begins.

Joseph Derek Barton (10) St Nicolas School, Abingdon

FEAR

The colour of white,
You gaze into my fiery eyes,
I look like the fire and the bitter, biting
Gale hangs around me like a shy child
Clinging onto her mother.
The aroma is like death
And the sour taste of the bitter acid
in a lemon.
The sound of a hollow scream,
Ringing round your head.
I feel like your hand in freezing water.
I taste like the stale and mouldy,
Sharp, disgusting bread
Which you hate.

Guy Bennett (10) St Nicolas School, Abingdon

MONSOON

Once a year,
Wet and windy,
It sheds its rain.

It pours down,
Warm and refreshing,
But also dangerous.

It pours and pours,
Causing great pleasure,
But also great sadness.

It floods cities,
Even countries,
And also kills.

It splits up,
Half east, half west.
It starts flooding.

For three months
It moves around,
Then leaves.

Michael Wallace (9) St Nicolas School, Abingdon

I SAW THE DRAGON

I saw the Dragon,
Huge and green,
Snarling madly,
Scaly and mean.

I saw the Dragon
Bend low to the ground,
With blazing eyes,
Staring and round.

I saw the Dragon,
With a horny beak,
Warty muzzle,
And bony cheeks.

I saw the Dragon,
Lift her head,
Let out a roar.
That could wake the dead.

I saw the Dragon,
Sniff the air,
Spread her wings,
Then fly back to her lair.

I saw the Dragon,
Enter the lair,
And turn her eggs,
With motherly care.

I saw the Dragon,
Stretch and yawn,
Then nestle down,
To await the dawn.

Hannah Salisbury (10) St Nicolas School, Abingdon

THE MONSOON

It seems to me like one great herd,
The rustling, grey sounds,
Of a forest far and still unheard,
With a rain dragon on his tail,
The fierce tiger roams India,
And way down south the children play.
In whispering winds,
And warm refreshing rain,
But far up north the elephant groans,
Torrential rain, an oasis of rain,
Ducks can swim along the road,
And boats can sail across them too.
But after three months the sun returns,
And so the monsoon goes,
It seems to me like one great herd.

Lauren Moore (10) St Nicolas School, Abingdon

THE MONSOON

The heavens open, the rain is here,
This thing happens once a year.
Rough winds whirl round and round.
Sweeping people off the ground.

Children in the refreshing rain,
People start to unblock the drain.
The water rises, it starts to flood,
It turns the earth into squidgy mud!

Richard Baker (9) St Nicolas School, Abingdon

SADNESS

Navy blue all around,
I'm lonely,
Sadness tastes like goat's cheese,
A lump comes to my throat.
Playtimes feel like a long struggle,
No-one to play with my own age.
Always seeing visions of Lizzy,
Wishing she was here.

Alice Alphandary (10) St Nicolas School, Abingdon

SLEDGING

Zooming through the glistening snow,
Flickering snow quickly blinding your eyes
So fast now
You have to close your eyes tight.
Half way down the hill
Watch out! Bump!
Whizzing through the winter air
Watch out! Snowball! Splat! It goes in your face
A frozen prickly thistle.
    S
    P
    L
    A
    T
We fall into the snow!

Alex Crosse (8) Shenington CE Primary School

THE DEWDROP

It hangs from a delicate, slender stem
Glistening in the morning light
Like a precious diamond - gem.
It hangs from a crane
Of silky green leaves
At the top the intricate flower
Is embroidered with magical patterns
Slowly the dewdrop falls
And it is gone forever.

Charles Saunders (8) Shenington CE Primary School

WINTER

The soft, swirling, sparkling snowflakes,
Drift slowly, slowly, slowly,
Down to the wilderness of white
Carpeting the busy roads,
But now the roads are mute.
The silver laced cobwebs
Sway in splendour in the morning breeze,
The crystal like icicles hang firm,
On the corner of an old forgotten shed,
And an icicle breaks loose!
It falls and pierces the soft flurry of snow,
The lonely snowmen have been completed
But, unfortunately they will not stand for long,
As the enchanted sun rises over the horizon,
The snowmen are now but a mere puddle on the bitter grass.
The snow has vanished!
But will it be back next year?

Nicholas Dexter (11) Shenington CE Primary School

DEATH FOR THE SNOWMAN

Me, the snowman
How scary it can be,
You don't know when
The sun will come out
Of those clouds up there.
I've got a hat on my head
And a scarf round my neck
To keep me cool!
Oh no! Here the sun comes.
It's not so long before my death.
It's not so long before everybody's death.

Nicholas Porter (8) Shenington CE Primary School

THE SEA

The scowling squalling waves lash out
Along the golden shore,
The roar and clap of stormy thunder clouds
Shatter the precious silence.
Fierce and vicious the splashing waves toss and turn,
Lapping onto the battered cliffs,
Covered by a moving carpet of snowy gulls.
As a seaman's pride is digested in the swirling sea,
The demolished wreck sinks deeply
Into the wailing waters.
The glistening sun sinks into the ferocious waves,
Bringing calm into the golden morning.
The profound waves lie calm on the shining shore,
And roll back to reveal gleaming coralled shells.

James Dexter (11) Shenington CE Primary School

THE SEA

The roaring sea comes rushing in
Crashing against the dark treacherous rocks.
White foam bubbles slide down the slippy rocks
From the last wave that came.
Boats bob up and down like a fishing float
As they sail over the angry sea waves.
The spray shoots up from the sea
Like a million gleaming crystals.
The howling wind roars like a lion
Whistling through the old light house door.
Tonight will be an exciting night.

Ben Young (10) Shenington CE Primary School

CATHERINE WHEEL

C atherine wheel lighting up the night
A blaze of glowing stars
T wirling in a blaze of red, orange, green and blue.
H urling around, kicking sparks to the earth
E ating sparks and spitting them out into the night
R acing in hope of cheers, cries and shouts
I n expectation from below.
N othing can stop it, even cold winds
E scaping softly as well as twisting.
W hee go the children in squeaky voices.
H ere come the sparks now,
E normous candles with sparks on their back
E very colour you can imagine
L ighting up the sky tonight.

Toby Lee (8) Shenington CE Primary School

NIGHT

Silently the night sleeps
On and on it snores
Darkness lurking around every corner
Everywhere still, silent
But petrifying.
The creaking trees mysteriously shudder
Breaking the errie silence.
The moon shimmers upon a meandering lake
Painting it ghostly silver to a touch.
Bats screech vigorously
Like screams from the burning dungeons of hell.
Hungry eyes peer sharply through the darkness
Seeking a dreamy, weary figure
To appear in its deadly territory.
The relentless wind keeps howling,
On and On and On.
Night stirs menacingly as though a warning
To every passer-by, to stay away, don't wake the sleeping night.
Weird shadows appear from nowhere, everywhere
Creeping stealthily like ghosts' footsteps
Nocturnal creatures, victims of the night
Hide timidly beneath
The brilliant silvery touch of moonlight.
The jewelled sky keeps staring,
Night brooding, moon stealing, dawn approaching.

Roberta Bullingham (11) Shenington CE Primary School

THE SEA

The sea is like a monster
swallowing everything in its forever changing path.
Why is it so tough and unforgiving
No-one will ever know
The sea is like the biggest and strongest giant
His sharp hands dragging back its victims
Out, far out into the dark deep sea
Until the tired waves release you
And discard you onto the golden beach
So quiet, so quiet, it scarcely breathes.

James Wasley (11) Shenington CE Primary School

MIRACLES

Miracles are everywhere,
Every morning the colourful cock crows
Each and every spring
Colourful flowers and blossoms appear all around,
All the time the living earth
Spins like an unstoppable,
Blue clear water in the long winding rivers
Is endlessly moving along,
Rain falls on the living world
Like a cold shower,
Flowers and trees are all different.
Each winter tiny snowflakes fall,
Every one different and unique,
To me these are all miracles.

Ricky Zito (10) Shenington CE Primary School

NIGHT

The silver moon shines down,
To make a moonlit path,
Along the still river,
A silver hedgehog scuttles along,
Sniffing out a dead mole or rat,
A flutter of wings rustle the trees,
A giant bird looking for its prey,
The gleaming silver path which is spread across,
The rippling white waters of the lake,
Is covered by the dark looming shadows,
Of the ghostly, monstrous trees,
Which break apart the silvery path.

Laura Wood (10) Shenington CE Primary School

FRUIT AND LEAVES

Autumn is the time for thanks,
and for apples to turn red and fall off trees.
Nuts fall off their little trees,
like jumping off a plane.
Autumn is the time for leaves to change
to yellow, orange and red, ready to
fall of the trees.
Leaves swirl and swish, round and round,
like a feather falling to the ground.
Yams start to grow in the field and
farmers start to pick the luscious fruits.
Pears and plums start to fall off
their trees.

Alexandra Thomas (9) Shenington CE Primary School

DAYDREAMS

I dream that I'm a princess
In a silk or velvet gown
I dream that I'm a queen
With a sparkling, jewelled crown
I dream that I have angel wings
That carry me away
To a land that's full of promises
You don't get every day.

I dream that there's a paradise
And only I know where
With trees of silver apples
And shining golden pears
It has a sparkling fountain
That spurts out lemonade
Frothy white and bubbly
In a giant wet cascade.

All these lovely daydreams
I dream of every day
Suddenly I'm a wizard
With lots of magic ways
And books of a great, great age
Then finally it fades away
And brings me back to reality
It's another boring school day.

Francesca Nunneley (10) Shenington CE Primary School

NIGHT

The church clock booms out its midnight tune,
The midnight secrets begin to loom,
Mystical creatures of the night,
Appear in the moon's clear light,
As night takes over.

Magic hidden in every leaf,
Trapped in midnight's frightening sheath,
Its secrets begin to unfold,
Its stories of darkness are told,
As night rules on.

The calling bats glide overhead,
Awaking the haggard and restless dead,
As they rise from their graves of lasting sin,
Welcoming, welcoming the darkness in,
As night continues.

The ghostly scene the night has made,
Silently begins to fade,
The morning sun enters the wakening sky,
Be happy for dawn is nigh,
Rejoice for night is dead.

Claire Pettit (11) Shenington CE Primary School

WINTER

The wind whispers and howls,
As swirling, floating white flakes
Fall from a grey sky.
The pavement is still and silent.
A million tiny snowflakes softly fall
From the grey, dark sky.

Philippa Wilkinson (9) Shenington CE Primary School

THE SEA

The silent sea washes the smooth sand.
And the gentle waves lap against the cold unyielding rocks.
A fish darts through the silky, silver seaweed.
And dolphins leap over the bouncing waves.
Golden shells lie on the seabed.
While the sealions play their splashing games
As the white, swirling foam grows and grows,
As the twirling wind grows angrier and angrier,
The waves seem to swallow the bewildered beach
Like a little child swallowing a fizzy drink.

Zoè Crosse (10) Shenington CE Primary School

THE SEA

The silent sea washes onto the silky shores
As the crisp white waves sparkle
In the endless moonlight
Cold pink crabs innocently crawl
Onto the warm sands
The waves chew hard on the rough rocks
Seagulls fish for their food
The cold night wind
Roars around the rusty rocks
As the great giant waves crash
Into the brittle caves
Leaving their ever repeating paths
Boats come to rest at the cold harbour
Welcoming them in from the murdering sea.

Lucy Poulton (11) Shenington CE Primary School

DAYDREAMS

I am floating peacefully
In a hot air balloon
And the hot summer sun
Lazily burns down on the spectacular landscape.

The refreshing, cool air
Blows softly over my pale face
And the birds sing happily
As they fly over the blue cloudless sky.

Far below a canal boat
Swiftly drifts down the shimmering waters
Of the canal, whilst lambs playfully
Leap over the luscious, green grass.

The fields far below are laid out
Like a patchwork quilt
And the frightened field mice scamper away
As a huge monster with grinding teeth approaches them.

Far away, the sea rolls against the sandy beach
Like a long, white ghost reaching out its grabbing hands
As the sky turns crimson and the sun sets
While looking at its glistening reflection in the calm waters.

Rosemary Pollard (10) Shenington CE Primary School

THE MIRACLE OF SPRING

The dancing squirrels,
Dance up the slippery slimy trees.
The snowdrops sprout out,
Making a wonderful lantern saying welcome to spring.
The acrobatic birds,
Put on a new performance,
As if to celebrate spring.
I think wonderful spring has melted the hard snow.

Richard Edwards (8) Shenington CE Primary School

DAYDREAMS

'He's listening' thinks Mrs Hartlett,
But no,
I'm swimming the broad Atlantic,
Or bungee jumping over the Thames.
I've won the lottery with
My lucky numbers.
I'm Michael Schumacher,
In my red Ferrari.
I'm boxing Mike Tyson,
Or drunk with lots of bubbly.
I'm on the moon
Or sitting in a
Big balloon,
Zooming through the clouds.
I'm the greatest lion-tamer
Or I'm Guy Fawkes
Trying to blow up the Houses of Parliament.
When I wake up everybody's gone to lunch!

Henry Lane (9) Shenington CE Primary School

THE SEA

The salt water in the aqua sea
Gets rough
Like a hungry dog
Going for the postman
Attacking menacingly the people on the golden sand
The cliff tops shine above the rest
While little children play gracefully
The children put shells to their ears
And hear the magic of the sea
Will it ever come to a lifeless end?
No!

Michael Cullen (11) Shenington CE Primary School

SNOWFLAKES

Snowflakes fall to the glittery earth.
They make a white tablecloth over the ground.
They slowly fall like feathers
And float on to the glittery branches.
They sparkle and shiver on my window sill.
Still they float and sparkle in the sky.
They float on to the icy pond and swiftly they have gone
They whisper to each other
While they swiftly drift down to earth.
The trees are like skeletons
And the world lies as still as a statue.

Rebecca Johnston (8) Shenington CE Primary School

DAYDREAMS

I'm going to buy a horse,
A champion jumper of course,
I'll brush his black coat every day,
I won't go to school, just play and play.

Daydreams, daydreams planning all my fun,
Daydreams, daydreams playing in the sun.

I'm going to Disneyland,
To shake Pluto and Mickey's hand,
I'll stay up late to see the fireworks show,
Sparkling, glittering, wonderful glow.

Daydreams, daydreams planning all my fun,
Daydreams, daydreams playing in the sun.

My rocket will take me off to the moon,
But don't worry mum I'll be back soon,
I'll jump and bounce and mess around,
I'll bring back a space pebble that I found.

Daydreams, daydreams planning all my fun,
Daydreams, daydreams playing in the sun.

My name is Captain Jake,
Gold and silver I must take,
I'll sail on the rolling sea,
We will have tea when we are free!

Daydreams, daydreams planning all my fun,
Daydreams, daydreams playing in the sun.

Edward Allsopp (9) Shenington CE Primary School

KITES

Kites drift through the sky
With a whistling wind
All lonely with a fluttering tail
Swooping up and down in the breeze
Gliding and humming in the bright blue sky
Bobbing and bouncing in the summer air.

Guillermo Sanchez (9) Shenington CE Primary School

MIRACLES

What is a miracle?
Maybe the streaming sun
Climbing above the distant horizon
Or the cheerful song
Of the swooping swallows.
The glowing of a shining lantern,
Standing quietly in the peaceful night.
Or the cry of a small baby,
Who has not yet seen the treasures
Of this wonderful world.

The changing of the mysterious tides
As the fishermen try their luck
Another time in the lonely waters,
Or the menacing roar of a lost tiger.
The beautiful pattern of a spider's web
As a glimpse of silver moonlight
Delicately paints the individual strands
Of a small fragile web,
Or even the birth of new, born chick,
Fluffy and golden yellow.
What would we do without miracles?

Laura Gaydon (11) Shenington CE Primary School

DESERTS

The searing sun beats down
On the silent desert floor
The golden sand is still
Only a bronze and green lizard
Hissing in the shimmering distance
Breaks the hazy stillness.

The sand hills stretch beyond the horizon.
All is still
The sun is forever beating down
On the endless burning sand.

Sophie Tisdall (10) Shenington CE Primary School

BUTTERFLY

Butterfly, butterfly dancing in the leaves
Colours red, pink and yellow
Shining like crystal stone.

Butterfly, butterfly winning every prize
Giving the swaying trees glowing beauty
And choosing the brightest of all the flowers.

Butterfly, butterfly, boasting about his
Gleaming colours red, pink and yellow
Butterfly, butterfly wonderful butterfly.

Jenny Berresford (8) Shenington CE Primary School

WINTER

Winter is here again,
Icicles hang like spears,
Flakes swirl in the wind,
As the cold settles,
Snow falls deeply,
Covering the ground,
Like my empty paper,
Waiting to be written on.

Robin Wilcock (10) Shenington CE Primary School

AUTUMN

A gentle haze of silver mist,
Floats across the diamond frosted fields.
The glistening silence is slowly broken
By a migrating flock of swooping swallows
Which drift across a magical sunrise.
A hasty gust of stubborn wind
Snatches away the gold trimmed crimson cloak
Belonging to a nearby oak tree.
A pheasant darts across a brown ploughed field
Moving like a feast of flame.
Mist swirls in wisps
Silent as ghost's footsteps.

Jennifer Allott (10) Shenington CE Primary School

RAIN

Pitter, patter goes the rain
Splish, splash it's pouring
Bang goes the rain on the roof.
Wallop!
Pitter, patter on the car.
Whoosh goes the wind and the rain.
Pitter, patter it's a shower
Shrump, shrump on the window
Drip drop it's nearly stopped.
      I love rain.

Joe Cooper (8) Shenington CE Primary School

SPARKLER

S piralling in the air
P laying in the night
A rching over excited voices
R eaching into the moonlit sky
K icking out other sparks to make it the King
L anding on the wet grass
E ar piercing noises landing in the moonlit sky
R eading the air which says 'get brighter'.

Jason Slade (8) Shenington CE Primary School

SUMMER BREEZE

I had wandered into a place where
willows crept into the water
and the stream plaited itself
over gravel banks.
The smell of a rose
brings beauty to my nose.
The moon is like a great balloon,
but it is on a string
to hold it down.
I listen to a bee who is -
as busy as a bee!

Kirsty McHardy (8) Uffington Primary School

PORCUPINE

He's in my bed,
Not in the shed.
I'll tie him up
I'll tie him down
I don't want him in my bed
I want him in the garden shed
So I tied him up
And tied him down
And put him in the shed
Now my bed is
Saved from the porcupine!

Louise Hibbard (8) Uffington Primary School

THE STREAM

Its waters
Trickling.
Big willows
Hanging over,
Reeds rustling.
The water
Stumbles over rocks
To make the patterns.
The stream holds secrets
As it flows away.
The bank
Holding its
Bursting waters.
Tadpoles taking swimming lessons.
When it rains
It makes ripples that get
Bigger and bigger.
When the rain stops
The stream shines
As the sun sparkles.

Louise Sworn (9) Uffington Primary School

WHITE HORSE

White horse
White horse
You are wonderful
White mane, starry eyes.
At night you come alive.
Dancing and prancing
Over the hill
Your silver shoes
glistening in the darkness
White horse
White horse
grazing in the moonlight
White horse
White horse
High up above
gazing down below
White horse
White horse
Carry me away
White horse.

Sophie Bowsher (8) Uffington Primary School

REMEMBRANCE

Wading through the poppy field,
Remembering those who died,
Gave their life for us who live,
In that awful war.

Every poppy in that field,
Could represent one person that died,
Wading through the poppy field,
Remembering those who died.

Caroline Woodhouse (11) Wantage CE Junior School

EVACUEE

She stood there waiting at the station,
She was picked but all on her own,
She felt so sad and lonely,
She wished that she could go home.

She went to where she was staying,
She was always bored,
She felt so miserable and unwanted
She had to behave she was warned.

She was glad when the war was over,
She could go back home,
She felt so pleased and excited
She wouldn't be all on her own.

Rebecca Partington (11) Wantage CE Junior School

WAR

I was sitting there all cramped up,
It was smelly and dark in the Anderson shelter,
I didn't know what to do,
I could hear the aeroplanes above the shelter,
At one time I thought they were going to drop bombs on us,
But luckily they didn't,
I was only nine years old.
School was off for another week,
I liked it at school and I made friends quickly,
If only there were no Germans,
If only there was no war.

There was an evacuee at our school,
His name was Jack,
When he first came to our country,
He crept along the playground,
Everyone laughed at him except for me and Tom,
After a while the teasing stopped,
The other boys and girls felt sorry for him,
If only there were no Germans,
If only there was no war.

Hannah Ewing (11) Wantage CE Junior School

THE PLANE WATCHER

I was watching one night,
Planes were flying,
Enemy planes searching.
Then I heard a humming sound,
Then guns were firing.
A big ball of flames was in the air,
And then the Germans were gone.

Christopher Alder (11) Wantage CE Junior School

WAR

The guns shoot
My brother and I are fighting
On the boat we get ready to fight.
We land on the beach.
Scared.
The Germans fire,
three hurt, one dead.
My brother and I dive for cover.
We get our guns ready.
Fear in our hearts, we get up.
We both fire, my brother shoots four.
We move closer with the army. It was not the same.
A bomb drops directly in the middle.
200 men dead.
My brother moves closer,
danger surrounds us.
Bang, Bang, Bang.
My brother hit the ground.
'No!' I shout.
I take him to cover.
'Fight for our country' he said.
'Leave me.'
Try to keep awake, but it is too late.
All is darkness.

Richard Rees (11) Wantage CE Junior School

AIR RAID

The air raids are horrible.
All the time all you hear is
Boom, boom, boom from outside the Anderson shelter.

Oh no! Oh no! screeched our neighbours.
We clambered out of our Anderson Shelter,
Only to find people crying and sobbing.
It was George our son.

The British Legion found us and lifted all the destruction.
Oh George was a mess.
He was taken to hospital.
We were told he was dead.
George, dear George our son.

Cheryl Shepherd (11) Wantage CE Junior School

THINKING

He can still hear the sounds of the planes roaring across the sky
dropping bombs
sirens sounding
people screaming
babies crying.
He was looking out of the window dismal and crying.
His heart was smashed with sadness and it crumbled inside him.
The stench of the rotting, lifeless bodies pierced his nose.
The bomb had destroyed his home.

Stuart Anderson (11) Wantage CE Junior School

THE EVACUEE

The evacuee was there, like a parcel,
Standing alone in the world,
Torn apart from family, friends,
Bewildered, lonely she shivers,
A suitcase in her hand.
She waits on the station.

Looking up at passers-by,
With pleading eyes, begging,
For another home to live in.
She imagines a house,
Warm and cosy, like home,
Smoke coming from the chimney.

A nice family like her own,
Sit and talk, make her warm.
She sits in an armchair
A cat sits on her lap,
There's a warm cosy fire
Someone take her in;
She wishes . . .

Lydia Haddrell (11) Wantage CE Junior School

IN THE WAR

When I stood on the airfield,
Waiting to get in the plane,
I felt really sad.
I thought of all the awful things,
Like death is very near, it makes me feel sad and scared,
I want to stop, turn and go back,
But now I think of all the people who need me to fight.
I will always fight for my country.

Andrew Bellis (10) Wantage CE Junior School

THE FUNNY WAR

Last night the street warden came round.
A glint of light peered through my curtains.
He knocked on the door and shouted loudly put that light out now.
I drew my curtains tightly closed,
So that not a glint of light could be seen.
I snuggled up in bed in the cold dark room,
With the night looming ahead.

At the beginning of school,
We all filed in putting our gas masks on the backs of our chairs.
Air Raid practice giggling as we disappear under our desks,
We all look a funny sight,
In our gas masks all black and white.
Thousands of Mickey Mouses all in one room,
A sea of Mickey Mouses all floundering around.
All parade down to the station giggling as we go,
Staring at the evacuees all jumping off the train.
I hope they will not be coming here,
But we are probably too near to Bristol.
All miserable and gloomy.
They had to leave their home, family and friends.
They do not give any thanks to the war.
I'm not scared of anything
I am not frightened of the war.

Sally Scholes (10) Wantage CE Junior School

THE DOGFIGHT

The plane ducked, bobbed, weaved,
The throbbing of an engine,
The tear of bullet against metal,
Fear lanced through his body,
Click, click, a gun reloading,
Two planes twisting, turning,
Gunfire all around,
Panic, despair, dread,
Two people battling for their countries,
Only one will survive,
Who? Why? Where?
The plane dived,
The scream of a man who knows what's next,
The whine of a nose-diving plane,
A crash,
An explosion,
All is quiet,
One man and one man only,
Flies back home tonight,
One man and one man only,
Will see daylight tomorrow,
And below, below
Is the wreckage of one plane,
A mangled German plane,
Lies scattered across a field of poppies.

Helen M Isserlis (11) Wantage CE Junior School

THE EVACUEE

She was evacuated.
I felt lonesome, sad, I felt like crying,
I saw her walk on to the train.
She blew me a kiss and I saw her wave.
It was not the same.

I spent the night thinking,
I wondered if she would ever come back.
I got evacuated too, I didn't meet any new friends.
I hated the country.
I missed her.
It was not the same.

I had news my Father had been killed,
I was told he bled to death with blood in his hair,
I went home, I saw my Mum,
But my Dad wasn't there,
And I never saw him again.

Joe Spray (10) Wantage CE Junior School

THE EVACUATION

The war came slowly.
When it came the boy named Tom from Manchester moved away.
He went to the country,
Lonely, cold and hungry.
When he got there he was teased and picked on.
He was so happy back in the city,
He had his mother, his father and his baby sister,
But for now he was lonely, cold and weeping.
Years passed and people stopped picking on him.
He was happy again.

Nicholas Clinch (11) Wantage CE Junior School

THE EVACUEE

He crept along the playground close to the wall
As he entered the classroom he heard a chorus of laughter
He weakened at the knees as the humiliation sank down his body
He saw an empty desk at the back of the room
He wished he was sitting there
So everybody would forget about him
But the teacher pointed to a desk at the front
Obediently he sat down
He felt like a coward, he was so frightened
If only he was at home safe with his Mom
If only he was earlier
If only he had been on time
At last the fear started to drain away
The lessons went so quickly
Then came the next problem
How would he know which children were evacuees
What should he do?
If only he had been earlier
If only he had been on time.

Laura Cavanagh (11) Wantage CE Junior School

SECOND WORLD WAR

I was a young boy in the Second World War,
Afraid of the bombs falling down,
Carrying my gas mask to school each day
and cheering when a German was killed.

I spent some nights in a shelter
Reading 'Boys Own' by candlelight,
Telling stories to each other
and sleeping when we could.

Jeremy Russell (11) Wantage CE Junior School

I AM NOT SCARED OF ANYTHING

I am not frightened of the war.
It's great fun, seeing planes dipping and diving.
I giggle a lot with my friends.
Ducking in and out of the shelter.
Every time we hear the air raid we run like the wind
to the shelter,
but we never run that fast.
I think it's ever so funny to duck under our desks.
We have to carry our gas masks everywhere.
They looked like a duck with a funny beak.
When the air raids come I shout 'Come on.'
I am not scared of anything.

Lynsey Pickett (11) Wantage CE Junior School

THE DUMP

Down by the dump,
with rusting things,
baked bean tins,
oil cans,
old frying pans.
Pollution is escaping,
Along with iron gating,
Stainless steel is wasting,
pecking through the dump,
I come across a lump,
that is my playground,
nothing but a waste ground.

Henry Callaghan (9) Wantage CE Junior School

THE EVACUEE

I stood at the station.
While people looked at me.
The people are giants to me.
They look at my name tag.
But no-one likes the look of me.
I am the only person left.
Everyone has gone.
Except for the teachers.
I feel lonely.

William Pattison (10) Wantage CE Junior School

REMEMBRANCE

R ations I get every week, on a Sunday, people are scared to look
    out of their houses.
E verywhere feels cold and sad, empty, anything could get blown up killed
    wrecked, I don't feel safe.
M inute after minute you're frightened dreadful things go through your head,
    'what if the Germans see a glimpse of light?'
E verywhere is pitch black, even in the house. Everywhere is black,
    you can't see a thing.
M any will surely be killed in the war, it's awful even thinking about it.
B rilliant times we had with the whole family together.
R oses die by the stream where we used to go fishing.
A ll are thinking, end the war.
N obody is coming out of their house anymore. It's depressing, seeing
    the streets bare.
C alendars we have passed through day after day, we wait.
E very day is a new day we will not give up hope.

Victoria Barrett (10) Wantage CE Junior School

WHEN I WAS EVACUATED

When war came I was evacuated.
I was cold, scared and frightened.
It was horrible. I wept and wept.
I heard footsteps behind me.
I quickly turned around.
It was just another poor little boy being evacuated.
He was weeping.
He was shivering and frightened.
I felt sorry for him like I felt sorry for myself.
I said, 'Hello.'
He looked up and said, 'Hello.'
But I could tell he was frightened and weak.
He had been weeping.
There were red marks down his cheeks,
And a bit of a tear still going down.
I felt like saying, 'Are you okay?'
But I knew he would not answer.
I did not say it.
He looked up and wept and wept.
More weeping boys and girls came.

Amy Pickett (10) Wantage CE Junior School

THE CRASH

Spinning, diving, heading for the sea.
Smoking engines *stop!*
Then we hit the sea.
The plane explodes into a fireball.
Swimming away bruised and battered.
Waiting for days, for someone to find us,
with no food, we starved.
Someone found us, cold and bewildered.

James Herkes (11) Wantage CE Junior School

EVACUEE

They stood there staring with critical eyes,
we were waiting to be picked.
Named and numbered,
homesick and lonesome,
I felt like a dog.

Everyone was being taken to a home
Except for me,
I was left with no friends
Nothing at all.
It was different here,
I wasn't special.

I was waiting for a long time,
The frost bit my fingers,
There was a feeling inside me,
I wanted to scream
Those strange accents,
They totally bewildered me.

I was lost without a home,
Then at last a teacher came,
She took me home,
She cared about me,
Someone cared,
I was safe.

Faye Richardson (11) Wantage CE Junior School

THE TRACK

As I got ready my blood was pumping hard,
Suddenly I heard a bang,
Off I went like the wind,
The stadium going round and round,
The track was endless.
The sun beating down hard
My legs about to fall off,
The torch looked like the sun,
As I finished I fall on the floor exhausted.

Jonathan Coxall (9) Wantage CE Junior School

CHRISTMAS EVE

Christmas Eve
St Nick is coming
With his sack of goodies!
I look out of the window
Suddenly!
Something quick
Comes across the field,
Something flying high,
It was old St Nick,
Who was coming!
I wanted to
Shout for joy
But I would
Wake the children
I went back to bed,
And dreamed of
Sugar Plums
dancing in my head!

Victoria Alice Green (9) Wantage CE Junior School

FROST

Icy day windy nights,
Stay in bed,
Before Jack frost bites,
Beautiful icicles,
Hanging by the window,
And the sun comes out
And the snow disintegrates.

Mark Cottrell (10) Wantage CE Junior School

FROM GREY TO TURQUOISE

She stands alone on the cobb wall.
The wind whistling around her,
The sea crashing on the shore.
Looking, looking she does nothing but look.
The sea's power begins to take effect,
Mesmerising her, drawing her in.
A gull screeches, she jumps,
Snapping her out of her hypnotic state.

The shingle on the beach grinds and tumbles down.
The sound is continuous and repetitive,
Stones whispering to each other.
The clouds part to reveal the sun,
With it comes a blue sky,
Which reflects in the sea,
Turning it turquoise instead of grey.
Gradually the sea calms and stills.

Catharine Birch (10) Wantage CE Junior School

THE TRACK

As I came through the doors
I looked at the people.
They looked back.
I felt anxious and scared.

The sky was as black as a lump of coal
The sun looked like cymbals
It was gold.
I walked to the start.
Everyone cheered and yelled,
I concentrated on the finish.

The gun shot, I had to go.
I was running and running,
Faster and faster,
My heart pumped madly,
My legs felt like jelly at this point,
Oh what if I fail, what if I trip?
I was now drawing level with somebody else
I said to myself I've got to win
I have! Oh I have!
The track seemed to go on forever,
I am so close to the finish,
I pass,
I have won!
I light the flame
It's now burning like the sun.

Amy Bridle (10) Wantage CE Junior School

ICE

Twisting, sliding down the snow goes
Magically, beautiful, splendidly,
It drifts into icyland,
Vanishing instantly in the bitter cold.
Unevenness, floating, drifting
Suddenly
They touch the porch,
Instantly turning into crystal knives.

James Ridgwell (9) Wantage CE Junior School

SPARKLING BLUE

Blue is the sky,
      on a summer's day.
Blue is sparkling sapphires,
      so people say.
Blue is the sea,
      shining out bright.
Blue turns the day,
      into the night.
Blue is gas,
      burning in the cooker.
Blue sees the future,
      like an onlooker.
Blue is an eye,
      looking all around.
Blue is a raindrop,
      falling to the ground.

Andrew Donovan (11) Wantage CE Junior School

THE TRACK

I was coming through the tunnel,
With my blood pumping around my body
And my hand and arm shaking around.
All the people made me nervous.

Starting the race in one moment.
My legs were shaking.
The gun shot! I started to run,
The wind rushing past me like a fan.

David Easton (10) Wantage CE Junior School

SEA MOODS

The sunlight glittering,
On the rolling waves,
As they surge up to the pebble beach,
But then they retreat back towards the horizon.

    The sea is an inky blue,
    It is poised and ready,
    Crashing on the shingle shore,
    Devouring the pebbles with its
    Rippled tongue.

As the sun begins to fade,
The stars are twinkling in the sky,
But still the sea rolls in and out,
Until the end of time.

Jocelyn Donnelly (11) Wantage CE Junior School

THE JUMP

Up ahead I see the track,
My mind is expanding
My heart is pumping wildly,
Sweat pours down my rough face.

The starter fires his dark black pistol,
Like a bullet I run down the red rubber track,
It seems never ending; the immense track,
I come to the white line.

I creep closer and closer,
I hurl myself in the air,
I land seventeen metres, and with great triumph,
I win gold in the long jump.

Thomas Malton (10) Wantage CE Junior School

THE ATHLETE

The long jump, a thrilling event
The sun steaming down on the ground
The crowd are thrilled at what they are going to see.

I line up on the track,
My legs feel like lead,
For not much sleep the previous night.

For my country I'm doing this
For my country I run up the track
For my country I land in the sand, second place.

Douglas Frost (10) Wantage CE Junior School

ICICLES

Slippery
Silver
Filigree
Crystal clear, vanishing
Wildness, whirling in patterns
Lying smoothly, muffling.
Magic fairy dust
Silver, fragile icy day.
Fairyland beautiful magical days.

Kirsty Jones (10) Wantage CE Junior School

THE WINTER POEM

Winter in January
Winter in February
Flakes white
Not like in summer
Summer is long, hot and weary
Winter is short, cold it doesn't hold
Then the next day snowflakes fall into sight
Melting at the touch of a hand
Coming down
Then suddenly gaining height
Snowmen slowly assemble
Snowballs fly through the air
Bedtime comes
It all becomes quiet once again.

David Stephen Finch (10) Wantage CE Junior School

THE TRACK

I come out on to the track,
All around the arena all the eyes
Are looking at me.
My blood is pumping all round my body.
I am waiting for the gun . . .
Bang! I am off the block in seconds,
My blood pumping even faster . . .
I am there, I've finished . . .
I wait, I've come first.
The gold medal is mine!

Matthew Hallam (10) Wantage CE Junior School

PLAYGROUND SOUNDS

When I went outside in the playground,
I heard some noises.
I heard footsteps strolling along the pathway.
Further down the road,
I heard builders,
Scraping their spades along the road.
The cars whooshing past,
Trying to get somewhere.
The birds were singing,
As a sign of spring.
We went outside Mrs Townsend's room,
I heard a desk close,
Very softly.

Ben Cole (10) Wantage CE Junior School

THE WAVEY SEA

The sea today is an exploding sea,
With thunderous waves,
Crashing against the shore,
Racing each other,
Pounding against the rocky shore,
The pebbles grinding each other to sand.

The waves tumbling down,
And splashing foam everywhere,
The sea today,
Seems very angry,
With wandering waves.

The scratching of seagulls,
Annoying nearly everyone,
The sea turning over seaweed,
This makes the sea a contrast of colour
Mixing well,
Then a giant wave crashes against the shore.

The twinkling waves,
Shining against the bright sun,
Trapped pebbles in little coves,
Whoosh! Whoosh! Whoosh!
Goes the spinning sea,
Roaring waves splashing everywhere.

Lapping waves at the shore,
While pebbles bang against the shore,
Still the giant race carries on,
With splashing foam,
Now the sea is on the turn,
Half waves everywhere.

Steven Vaux (11) Wantage CE Junior School

THE BONFIRE

That time of year comes round again,
Start collecting the wood and leaves,
Cook the toffee, fudge and sweets,
Ready to toast in the dying embers.

We go out into the November darkness,
With matches, firelight and sparklers,
Light the fire and watch it roar,
Burning the Guy up to the stars.

The sparklers burst and make a rainbow,
Colours of magic, leaping and dancing,
The twinkling light cascading down,
Then dying away like a leaf in autumn.

Next we have the sticky marshmallows,
Put them on sticks and hold them tight,
They go brown and golden in the flames,
Hot to the touch but lovely to eat.

Then we dance around the bonfire,
Watching the fountain get lower,
We poke the potatoes, 'are they done?'
And huddle round the cosy blaze.

Caroline Moore (11) Wantage CE Junior School

THE SEA'S MOODS

The sea rears its head and mane
Crashing it down on the yellow sand,
Retreating nursing a bruise, it forgets and does it again
As it retreats a second time,
It steals some pebbles,
But they are too heavy,
So it drops them and retreats again
Once again it lunges forward,
This time it drags sand with him.

A seagull dives and brings back nothing
It screeches and dives again,
Into turquoise waters, it surfaces with a fish in its beak.
The sea roars for its treasure back,
But alas the gull has eaten it,
Then the sea grows restless,
Pacing back and forth,
All wise birds keep out of its way.

Then the sea gets angry,
And smashes itself on the rocks,
Pointlessly bashing itself again and again,
Urged on by wind and rain.
Driven by fear of thunder and lightning,
Then the storm goes leaving a tired sea,
The sea sleeps snoring softly,
Until the morning comes,
When it is angry again.

Mark Harris (11) Wantage CE Junior School

ANOTHER WORLD

The turquoise depths,
of sapphire and emerald,
the salty sea air,
spraying me with a
tangy smell and touch.

Pebbles, crashing together
the tumbling and rumbling,
sounds they make together.
They'll never be free,
always being dragged in
and out by the tide.

The sea is full of seaweed,
seaweeds in all different colours,
browns, greens and reds.
They mingle with each other.
Making new colours.

A crab boring its way,
through the sand.
Limpets stuck fast to the
rocks, clinging on for dear life.
Little fish and crabs scuttle
and swim through the seaweeds
they hide away till the tide
returns . . .

Helen Oakes (10) Wantage CE Junior School

PLAYGROUND SOUNDS

I went exploring for sounds in the playground,
First we wandered to the copper beech,
We stood there in stunned silence,
Then we heard a sharp bleeping!
It was a van reversing,
We waited for a moment,
In a chorus the tweet, tweet of birds.

The clattering of feet against stone,
As we walk to the white school gates,
We listen for a moment,
Then the sound of a car,
A breezy, undisturbed sound,
Some noise is made by a metal spade hitting stone,
A kind of clang, then a scrape like a crow cawing,
The distant sound of people conferring,
The slamming of a door closing.

The chattering noise of children,
But the teacher booms her loud voice,
All sounds cease from the classroom,
Crumpling of books,
As we slump slowly back to school.

Ben Carter (11) Wantage CE Junior School

WHAT IS BLUE?

What is blue?

Blue are waves,
as they crash against the rocks.
Blue is your eye
like the glistening sky.

Blue is your ink,
as it touches the paper.
Blue is water
as you swim,
Blue is your pencilcase,
as you finish with it.

Shaun McNamara (11) Wantage CE Junior School

FIREWORKS NIGHT

Bonfires blazing on fireworks night,
Flickering in the moonlight.
Catherine wheels whizzing round,
A fountain of sparks showering the ground.

Shining fireworks falling down,
Coating the ground in a dazzling gown.
Shooting stars way up high,
Illuminating the sky.

Now the bonfire stops burning,
No more Catherine wheels are turning.
Midnight chimes: a new day breaks,
Potatoes on the fire are baked.

Auriol Proudfoot (11) Wantage CE Junior School

THE MYSTERIOUS GIRL

The girl's wispy hair,
Blowing in the salty sea air.
She's watching,
Watching the waves lapping up and
down the shore.
The frothy white foam brushing the
pebbles,
But whispering as it goes.
She gets off the sharp rocks,
Onto the smooth pebbly shore.
The auburn sun beams down on her,
She steps down to the cool
Refreshing water.
The breeze makes the waves ripple,
around her feet.
The sea suddenly starts to get
raging,
Crashing against the rocks,
The girl quickly runs out on
tiptoe.
Waves beating across the shore,
Turning the smooth, smooth pebbles
over.
The sea is lonely without a
friend,
It wants someone to step into his
waves.
The girl's wispy hair,
Blowing in the salty sea air.

Kate McIntyre (11) Wantage CE Junior School

THE MOOD-SWINGING SEA

As I sit on the cobb,
I listen to the sea.
The waves crashing,
The wind blowing.
As the sea goes in and out.

I can smell the salty sea,
And the seaweed weeping.
I can smell the crabs,
Tumbling in with the sea.

I can see,
The sea ripples getting bigger
As it grows.
I can see cliffs crumbling,
Rocks cracking.
And the waves slapping.

I can hear the sea,
Grinding the pebbles and rocks.
I can hear the wind,
Howling through rocks and caves.
I can hear moans of the sea.

The waves can be brisk,
As fast as the wind.
The waves can be calm,
Like a summer's night.

The bottom of the sea,
Is a different world.
There's seaweed lapping over.
And fish which live in cracks.

The sea is a mood-swinging,
But living world.
A wonderful different world.

Alison Barber (11) Wantage CE Junior School

THE MYSTERIOUS SEA

The sea sapphire blue,
Turquoise in the depths.
The long inky black coast line
Stretching for miles.
Wheeling screeching gulls
Above the tiny insignificant
Fishing boats of Lyme Regis.

As I approach the pearly white
Breaking waves,
I smell fish, seaweed,
Fresh salty sea air.
The waves lap in and out
Turning pebbles around.
The waves crashing and slapping
Against the Cobb Wall,
White spray rising up the stone.

Now the wind has gathered
Up its courage and is howling
Around barnacle covered rocks.
The sea swishes in and out
Of the yellow grey shore
In its restless, uneasy way.
The wavy seaweed being pushed,
Pulled by the racing bullying sea.

The sea's white breaking waves
Ripple slowly up the beach,
Swaying but not staying!
The pebbles sigh, all is quiet,
Except for the dark mysterious,
Rumbling, tired sea.

Elizabeth Berrett (11) Wantage CE Junior School

A WORLD OF ITS OWN

I see,
    The emerald green waves,
    Rushing towards the rocks,
    Pearly white horses break,
    Then retreat from the shore,
    Calm turquoise, ripples mingle,
    In amongst the patchworked pebbles.

I hear,
    The lapping, rushing wavelets,
    Then colossal waves crashing,
    Smashing against the boulders,
    Seagulls screeching while they soar
    Their graceful bodies bob up and down

I feel,
    So unimportant against this vast expanse,
    It looks so angry, brisk and raging,
    Devouring the restless shingle,
    As it uneasily whisks away the darting fish.

I smell,
    The distant waving seaweed,
    Swaying in the undersea world,
    Fish lying dead, rotting away,
    Their lives short but wonderful,
    Salty waters ebbing and flowing,
    All these odours are natural.

    The sea has a world of its own.

Naomi Ryland (11) Wantage CE Junior School

THE BONFIRE

There it sits, ready to be lit.
All of a sudden, there's a whoosh!
The bonfire is lit!
Crackling, whizzing, sparks are
Flying.
Now there are glittering stars,
Booming sounds.
The fireworks are off.

First the screamers,
Now the flashing Catherine wheels,
All the colours are like a rainbow.
Now there are happy smiling faces.
It's the sparklers,
In their hands.

Mark Clements (11) Wantage CE Junior School

THE CRASHING WAVES

The rushing, crashing waves,
Beating the pebbles against each other.
Violent, roaring, pounding waves,
Like a battle between land and sea,
Swiftly crashing against the land.
A loud bang,
Then another,
Then it goes quiet.
The land slips away into the sea's mercy.
The sea is powerful.

Daniel Humphries (11) Wantage CE Junior School

PLAYGROUND SOUNDS

I can hear the sound of a screeching car,
As I stand in the playground listening hard,
I hear chairs scraping and teachers talking,
When I turn round I find more sounds.
Water gurgling down a drain,
An engine going on, off and on again,
I hear people talking about this and that,
A car starting and people walking.
Some people say that the playground is restful
I agree, but not for silence,
The noises do wonders for rest!

Timothy Kennington (10) Wantage CE Junior School

PLAYGROUND SOUNDS

I stood listening,
To the birds in the trees,
I heard bustling,
Cars whizzing by in the distance,
Fading slowly away.

I heard men working,
They were dragging spades,
Drilling in the road,
Shouting and calling voices.

People slamming doors,
Then walking off,
You can hear the footsteps,
From a hurrying man,
The playground is still and peaceful now.

Jessica Rolls (10) Wantage CE Junior School

THE ENCHANTED SEA

As I stand on the cobb,
At Lyme Regis,
I hear the sea,
Pounding against the rocks.
Sapphire blue waves,
Crashing and lapping,
To the shore.

Emerald is the seaweed,
Bathing in the sun,
Until the sea picks it up,
And rides off into the sunset.

The pebbles grinding,
As the sea tumbles over them,
Fossils submerging,
From the sea-bed,
All the time.
Ammonites, belemunites,
You never know,
What you may find.

I feel calm and gentle,
As I watch the sea,
With its lapping waves
And whispering noises,
An entrancing, playful sea.

Laura Bowles (11) Wantage CE Junior School

THE LION ROARS

The blue sea crashing
        against the rocks
pebbles crashing together,
seagulls screeching in the sky,
lapping and racing the waves go,
like a lion roaring.

Smooth pebbles yellow and pink,
all different colours,
green and blue is the sea,
waves brushing the rocks in.

Star yellow is the sun,
shining on the sea,
the sea is running up the beach,
slapping on the cobb,
waves tumbling over each other.

Silver grey is the clouds,
shaped clouds are funny,
moods of the waves are very mixed
rocks rocks rocks crashing,
people sailing across the sea.

A cloudy day is very mad,
gentle but not so rare,
the lion's still roaring,
up the wall,
of the cobb.

Ships are sinking,
sand flying around,
crabs biting people,
people are sighing because,
the sunset is near.

Stevie Rutter (11) Wantage CE Junior School

THE SEA

The calm sapphire sea,
   And the emerald green waves,
With the pearl white cloud,
   Drifting over the sea.

The sound of lapping waves,
   And rippling of the sea,
As the calm gentle water,
   Moves swiftly in and out.

The midnight blue of the sea
   Raging and roaring,
And the grey misty night,
   With the howling wind.

The rolling waves,
   Crashing against the rocks,
And the rushing of the sea,
   As it grinds up the pebbles.

Kieran Wheeler (11) Wantage CE Junior School

LYME'S BEACH

As the waves are
coming in,
I can hear them,
Crashing and swishing,
With the opal white froth,
Bubbling as the waves,
are crashing against the rocks,
I can hear the shingle,
Chiming as they hit each other,
While they hastily,
Run up and down the beach,
The seagulls are shrieking,
And eating cold chips,
I see people over at Black Venn,
Crunching their way,
Through the pebbles,
Seeking out fossils.

Stuart May (11) Wantage CE Junior School

INFORMATION

We hope you have enjoyed reading this book - and that you will continue to enjoy it in the coming years.

If you like reading and writing poetry drop us a line, or give us a call, and we'll send you a free information pack.

Write to

        Young Writers Information
        1-2 Wainman Road
        Woodston
        Peterborough
        PE2 7BU